# The Circle of Fifths

visual tools for musicians

Philip Jackson

The Circle of Fifths: visual tools for musicians



ISBN 979-10-95580-00-3

Comments and suggestions are welcomed by email. They will help us to eliminate any errors and improve later editions.

email : fifths@le-theron.com

Website : https://le-theron.com

# Preface

When I was learning to play a musical instrument and the associated musical theory, the mass of factual detail given to me concerning intervals, scales, chords and harmony did not always seem to form a coherent entity. The relationships between the various elements were not always evident.

Naturally, that reflected mainly on my inability to understand all those relationships arriving in too short a space of time. Perhaps too, the teachers were treading a well worn and familiar path which did not fit well with my aspirations.

Later when I moved towards techniques of improvisation, I found difficulty in assembling these many facts into a structure which would enable rapid recall. I could often remember where to find the facts rather than the facts themselves. It appeared that my visual memory was dominant.

The circle of fifths came to be the visual crutch I needed and on which I could rely as a basis for seeing the structural coherence of multiple aspects of music. Time after time, I found that I was able to associate a series of facts with the circular representation of fourths or fifths.

I have assembled these ideas into a small tool-kit which I hope will help many others with their learning and understanding of musical theory and its application in performance. This book is not intended as a basic course in music theory and it is expected that the reader will already be acquainted with scales, intervals, chords and chord progressions.

Following suggestions from many students, I have prepared sets of exercises to help reinforce the learning. These are now available as workbooks in the Visual Tools for Musicians Series. References to these exercises have been added in each chapter where relevant. I have also prepared some additional material which is available as an optional free download. See the Resources section in Appendix E.

Please take and adapt for your own use those ideas that you find most useful.

Philip N. Jackson, 2021

# Table of Contents

# 1 - Introduction

Our intention is to make this book a practical kit of tools for visualising those aspects of music where the brain (of some of us) can get easily left behind and overwhelmed by the task at hand. It is expected that these tools will be of especial interest to musicians involved in improvisational musical genres, jazz, jazz-folk fusions.

To make the best use of this book, the reader should have an understanding of scales, chords and intervals but in most cases a small recap of such material is provided where thought relevant.

We will not hesitate to simplify and this will the most often be evidenced by the re-spelling of note names : C♯ will become D♭, B♭♭ will become A, F♯♯ will become G. These are but a few examples of simplification which might shock theorists but eases the job of the practising musician. Key and scale may well be used interchangeably – more practical.

Experience in teaching these ideas has shown the benefit a series of practical exercises can give to students to help their understanding and to improve their visualization of the methods used. To this end, we have prepared workbooks of exercises in three volumes which follow the same layout as this book. Details are provided in the Other Books section.

## Conventions regarding chords

### Triads with perfect fifths

- The perfect major triad will be represented simply by the letter name of the root note. C major triad will be simply written as C.
- Minor triads will be represented like this : Cm

### Triads with altered fifths

- Augmented triads will be represented as : Caug
- Diminished triads will be represented as : Cdim

### Seventh chords with perfect fifths

- Major seventh chords will be represented like this : Cmaj7
- Dominant seventh chords will be shown as : C7

- Minor seventh chords : Cm7
- The minor triad with major seventh : Cm.maj7

### Seventh chords with altered fifths

- the augmented triad with major seventh : Caug.maj7, Cmaj7♯5 , Caug9
- the augmented triad with minor seventh (altered chords) : C7♯5
- the half-diminished seventh : C⌀ or as Cm7♭5
- the diminished seventh : Cdim7

## Conventions regarding scales

We shall use the major scale as the point of reference for all scales and modes and for harmonic analysis, the degrees of the major scale will be represented by Roman Numerals using upper case to represent notes having a diatonic major third (within the scale) and lower case for notes having a diatonic minor third.

Using C Major as an example of the harmonisation of the major scale, we have :

| C | D | E | F | G | A | B |
|---|---|---|---|---|---|---|
| I | ii | iii | IV | V | vi | vii |

This concurs with the accepted harmonisation of the major scales.

### Melodic analysis – some remarks

When deriving a chord or another scale, we shall respect the convention of using as the point of departure the major scale commencing with the same tonic note name. In this case, we shall use Arabic numerals. Some examples are listed below :

C major triad consisting of notes C - E - G will have a melodic analysis based on the C Major scale : 1 3 5.

C minor triad consisting of notes C - E♭ - G will have a melodic analysis based on the C Major scale : 1 ♭3 5.

C dominant seventh chord consisting of notes C - E - G - B♭ will have a melodic analysis based on the C Major scale : 1 3 5 ♭7.

C major pentatonic scale consisting of notes C D E G A will have a melodic analysis based on the C Major scale : 1 2 3 5 6.

## About the circle

The circle of fifths is also known as the cycle of fifths or the circle / cycle of fourths. The interval of a fourth is, of course, the inversion of the fifth. The circle can be found drawn with flats on the left-hand side and sharps on the right or the other way round.

In earlier periods when much of musical harmony was triad based, the cycle of fifths was perhaps a more appropriate name in the sense that it referred to a progression or motion to and from the primary triads constructed on the first, fourth and fifth degrees of a major scale. This motion acted as a cadential element serving to establish the tonal context or colour of the music. The fourth degree is a fifth below the tonic and the fifth degree is a fifth above the tonic. So, these degrees can be viewed as bracketing the tonic in a cycle of fifths and indeed, on our circle of fifths they are either side of the tonic.

For this book, I have adopted the convention of naming it the 'circle of fifths' and drawing it with sharps increasing in the clockwise sense. Fear not ! Once you have worked with the circle for a little time, you will not have any difficulty drawing it the other way round or even visualising it either way in your mind's eye.

So we will consistently show the circle as you see it below, in Figure 1.1, with a series of ascending fifths (or descending fourths) in the clockwise sense and descending fifths (or ascending fourths) in the anti-clockwise sense. We will also consistently place C at the 12 o'clock position, whether it is the tonic of the scale or not.

In earlier times, the succession of twelve perfect fifths did not cause the circle to close on itself. There was a small excess of approximately a quarter of a semitone and this was known as the Pythagorean comma. The 'circle' was more precisely a first turn of a helix. The adverse effect of transposing a piece of music into remote keys could be clearly heard.

Over the centuries, many ways were tried to eliminate this problem and these culminated in our equal tempered system where the octave is maintained as a doubling of the sound's frequency between notes of the same name and the 'frequency space' between these two notes is split into twelve equal intervals. The size of each semitone is thus equal and defined by the factor $2^{1/12}$.

The result is that the Pythagorean comma has been eliminated, the circle has been flattened and is no longer a first turn of a helix but the price to be paid is that each of our equally tempered fifths is very slightly flat compared with the natural ratio of 3:2. The advantage is that we now have no difficulty in transposing a piece of music into any key and having it sound right.

You can see further notes on the overtones and the harmonic series in the appendix A.

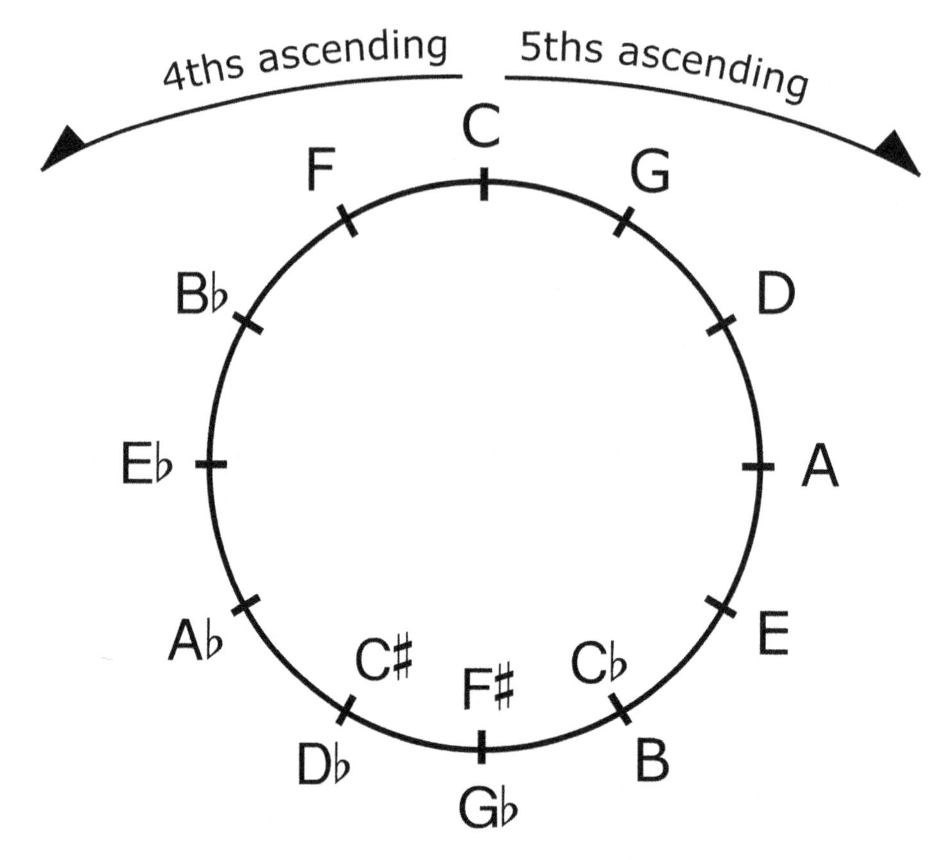


Figure 1.1: The Circle of Fifths

Where the diagram shows 'fifths ascending', it could also be marked 'fourths descending'. Similarly, 'fourths ascending' is the equivalent of 'fifths descending'.

I also show the circle with C at the top (the 12 o'clock position) but this too, is only a convention. You may find it more convenient to place the tonic of the scale currently under consideration at the 12 o'clock position in order to have a constant image of the scale degrees which will be introduced in Chapter 2.

All twelve notes of the chromatic scale have their place on the circle: the seven notes A to G and the other five are conventionally shown as flats – A♭, B♭, D♭, E♭, G♭. But these may require re-spelling as G♯, A♯, C♯, D♯, F♯ to conform to a more general usage.

The positions on the circle can represent notes in a scale or the scales themselves according to circumstances. Rather than any other model, we are using the circle as a spatial model to represent notes as a neutral pitch class. Other models could make similar representations but in a more tonal context. One such model could be a linear representation of fifths where different spellings of the same pitch would be placed differently, for example G♯ and A♭. Their respective positions would show different tonal relationships with a second pitch like C.

Such a model is more appropriate for analytical purposes but for practical musicianship, for playing and improvising, I prefer the circle where we are comparatively neutral about the difference between G♯ and A♭. For a discussion of the various spatial models, I recommend section 5.2 of David Temperley's book, *The Cognition of Basic Musical Structures*, published by the MIT Press.

Note that I have shown alternative spellings for some of the scales at the bottom of the circle. You will need to take the spelling which is appropriate to the context. Examples will be explained in other chapters.

## Learn the circle

The essential first step to possessing the circle in your mind's eye is to learn to draw it from memory.

- Draw a circle – freehand will do
- draw a dot in the estimated centre of the circle
- mark the four cardinal points : 12 o'clock, 3 o'clock, 6 o'clock, 9 o'clock ; try to keep the 12 and 6 marks opposite each other, on a diameter of the circle, similarly with the 3 and 9 o'clock marks
- draw in the remaining marks, using the central dot to try to keep opposing marks aligned on a diameter
- write in the names of the fifths
- write in the names of the degrees

After a few rehearsals, you'll be able to draw the circle in any order and in either direction.

Memorizing the circle is fundamental to all that follows in this book and is so important that we have prepared some pages of blank circles as a free download. See the Resources section in Appendix E.

Exercise material on the contents of this chapter is available in *The Workbook: Volume 1 – Early Steps.*

Notes

# 2 - Major Scale Degrees

Taking C Major as a first example, Figure 2.1 shows the degrees, or rank of the notes, of the major scale with the tonic, first degree, I at the 12 o'clock position.

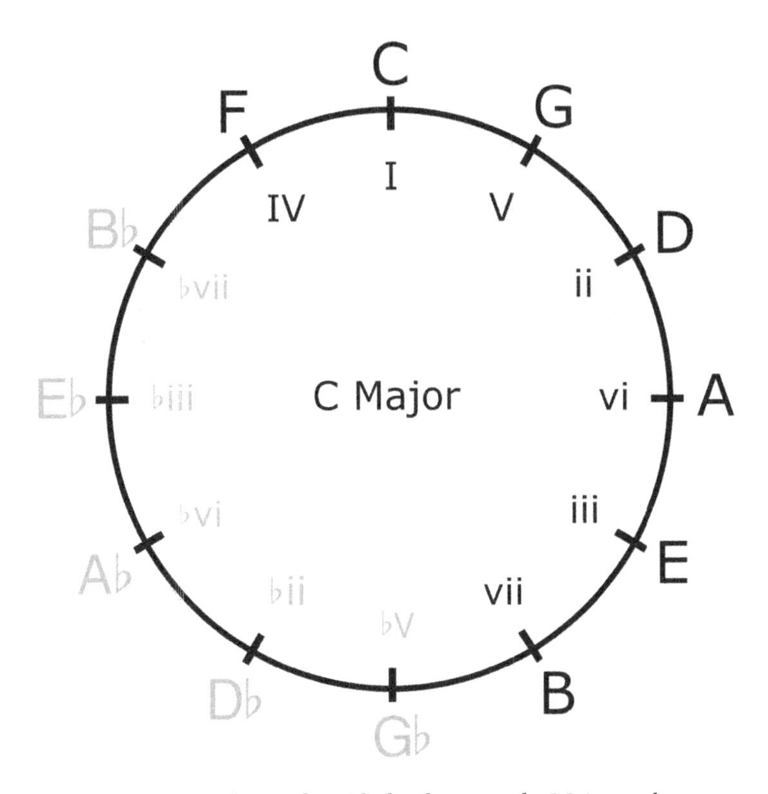


Figure 2.1: the circle with the degrees of a Major scale

The diatonic degrees have their names and degrees marked more boldly. The other five steps on the circle are shown fainter and they are altered, non-diatonic, degrees shown in Figure 2.1 as flattened degrees but they equally be respelled as sharps depending on the context. Together, the seven diatonic degrees and the remaining five steps represent the entire chromatic scale. [1]

Two further examples are shown in the following diagram, with the scale degrees rotated so that the I degree is lined up with the tonic of the scale. I have preferred to keep the note names in the same position and to mentally rotate the scale degree references. I find this way easier to recall when dealing with chord progressions.

1 See Appendix B, page 87 for semitone progressions

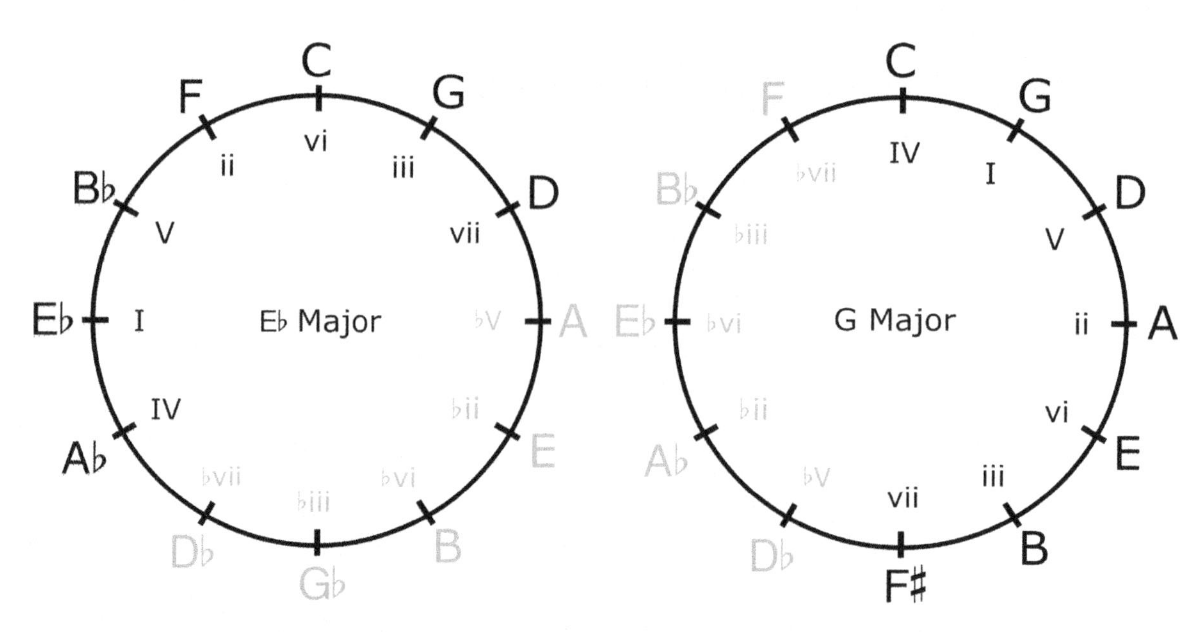


Figure 2.2: scale degrees for E♭ Major on the left and for G Major on the right.

You may prefer to do the opposite – keep the scale degree references as shown in Figure 2.1 above and to mentally rotate the names of the notes to get the tonic to align with I at the 12 o'clock position. This is not our approach in this book.

Exercise material on the contents of this chapter is available in *The Workbook: Volume 1 – Early Steps.*

# 3 - Sharps and Flats

The circle of fifths provides a convenient visual way of remembering both the number of sharps and flats in the major scales and their order of appearance in each key. We will not consider the cases of double sharps nor of double flatted notes. In general, we believe that for a practical musician, respelling key signatures to avoid double sharps or flats will provide a simpler and more easily read notation.

## The sharp keys

First, the number of sharps in each major scale : starting with C Major which has no sharps and proceeding clockwise around the circle, we have G Major scale with one sharp in its key signature. Each succeeding Major scale has one additional sharp up to C♯ Major which has a sharp on all seven of its notes.

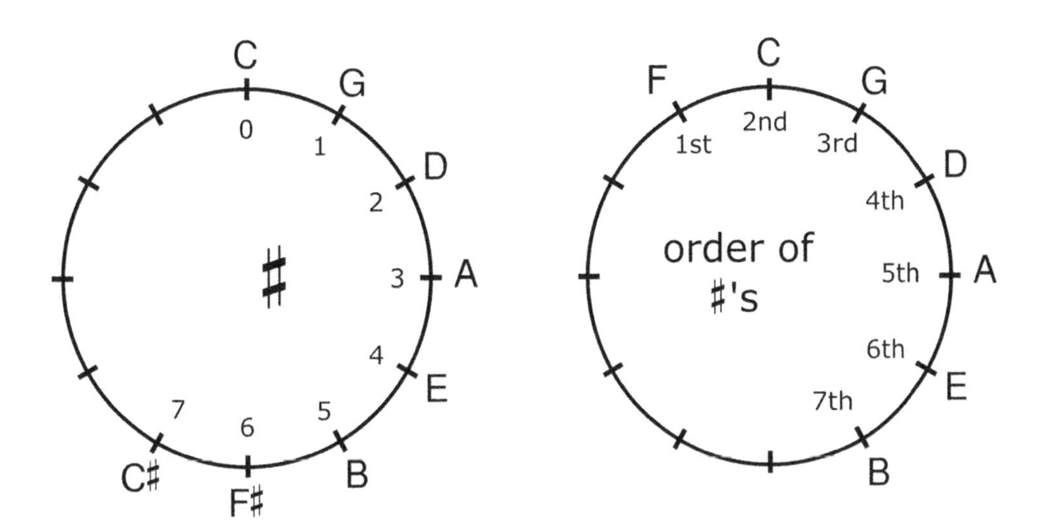


Figure 3.1: the number of sharps in major scales and their order of appearance

So, E Major has four sharps in the order : F♯ , C♯ , G♯ , D♯ . The last note to receive a sharp is B and this will complete the seven for C♯ Major.

Beyond C♯ Major, the four positions left vacant on the circle would be completed by G♯ Major, D♯ Major, A♯ Major and E♯ Major. Each of these would require at least one double sharp note and we will not consider that case here.

## The flat keys

The order of appearance of flats is often taught as the reverse of the order of sharps as in the following diagram. The order of the flat notes is : B E A D G C F.

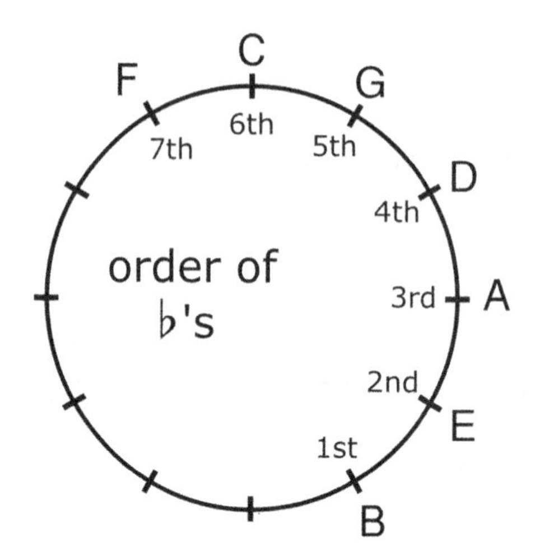


Figure 3.2: the order of the flats

B is the first note to receive a flat, E the second and so on in anti-clockwise fashion to F which is the last note to receive a flat.

I would suggest that it is easier to consider the order of the keys to which the flats are applied and how many flats are in each key signature. Figure 3.3 shows the distribution on the circle of fifths of the flat major scales together with the number of flats in each scale.

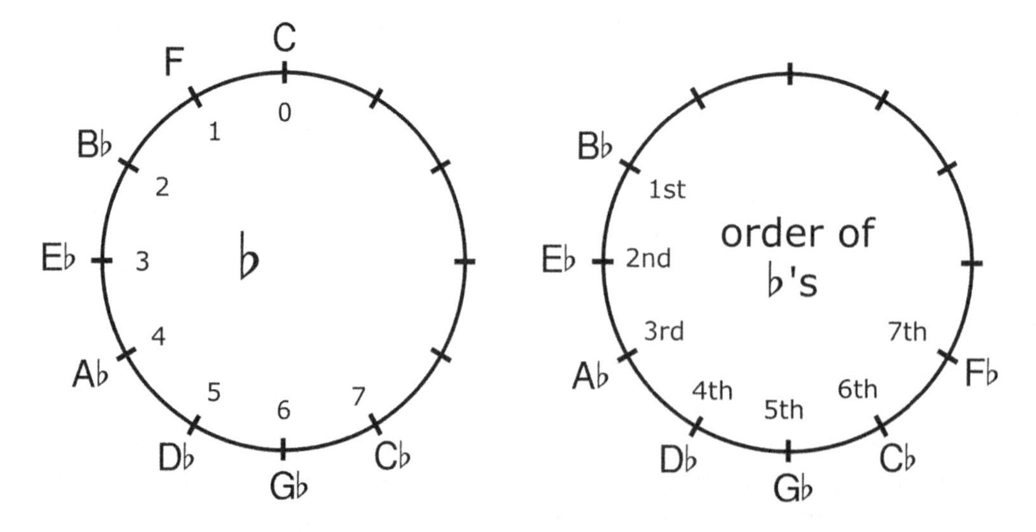


Figure 3.3: the number of flats and their order of appearance

You will have to remember the starting point which is 1 flat for F Major. Then move up in fourths (anti-clockwise) to C♭ Major which has all seven notes as flats.

Further progression in the same direction will require the use of double flats (♭♭). For example, the next step up a fourth from C♭ Major will be F♭ Major (see Figure 3.3) which will have the following pitch values :

F♭ G♭ A♭ B♭♭ C♭ D♭ E♭

We will limit ourselves to the use of single flats. Double flats can always be respelled : B♭♭ is the same pitch and sound as A. For performance, this is the most practicable method. In a first instance, this will give us a respelled scale :

F♭ G♭ A♭ A C♭ D♭ E♭

Although this poses no problem for performance, it will be an unwelcome spelling for the purist because an essential feature of a diatonic major scale is to use all seven note names. So the better solution is to respell the whole scale :

E F♯ G♯ A B C♯ D♯

Thus E Major is an enharmonic equivalent of F♭ Major and provides a simpler expression for the musician because it avoids double flats.

## Further resources

Further material is available to help with practical issues involving choices of keys and the implications for transposing instruments playing together. The practical use of the circle of fifths in transpositions is discussed in Chapter 13.

Some more notes are available as a free download. Among these, you will find a short note on some practical implications of the choice of keys and a note on the spelling of the main keys in both major and minor variants. See the resources section in Appendix E.

Exercise material on the contents of this chapter is available in *The Workbook: Volume 1 – Early Steps.*

Notes

# 4 - Intervals

The first hurdle with counting intervals, possibly only for those with a technical or scientific background, is to remember to count the starting note as '1' and then to continue for the necessary number of note names. For example, to find the note a major third up from G, start with G as 1 and then A is 2 and B is 3. So B is a major third (two tones or whole steps) up from G.

I found that it helped me to have a picture in my mind of the different intervals rather than having to count forwards or backwards through the alphabet – especially backwards. Counting backwards was so frustrating to me that I would rather take the inversion of the interval in order to be able to count forwards.

Using our construction of the circle as we defined it in Figure 1.1 of chapter 1, we can now split the intervals into three groups :

1. those that ascend in a clockwise direction (descend anti-clockwise)
    - major intervals
    - perfect fifths
2. those that ascend in an anti-clockwise direction (descend clockwise)

- minor intervals
- perfect fourths

3. the tritone – this is more easily imagined on the diameter and is discussed further in chapter 6.

The intervals in the second group are the inversions of those in the first group. The inversion of the tritone is still a tritone.

## Major intervals and the perfect fifth

These ascend in the clockwise direction and descend in the anti-clockwise sense :

- the major intervals (major second, major third, major sixth, major seventh)
- the perfect fifth

Figure 4.1 shows how these intervals are to be found on the circle, starting from C in the case of this illustration. A major sixth up from C is A (the third step up in the clockwise direction). A major third down from C is A♭ (the fourth step down from C).

Certainly, you can start from any note, and a major third above that note will be found by taking four steps round the circle in the clockwise sense. Thus a major third up from A is C♯ (a respelling of D♭).

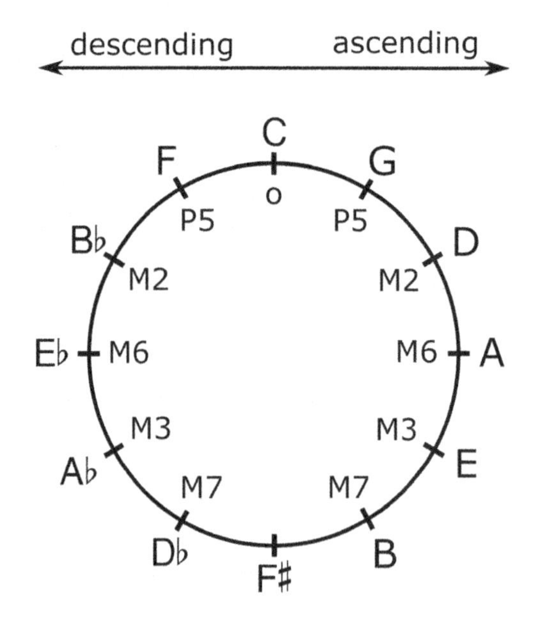


Figure 4.1: major intervals & perfect 5th

## Minor intervals and the perfect fourth

These ascend in the anti-clockwise direction and descend in the clockwise sense :

- the minor intervals (minor second, minor third, minor sixth, minor seventh)
- the perfect fourth

Figure 4.2 shows how these intervals are to be found on the circle, starting from C in the case of this illustration. A minor sixth up from C is A♭ (the fourth step up in the anticlockwise direction for minor intervals). A minor third down from C is A (the third step down from C, clockwise sense for minor intervals).

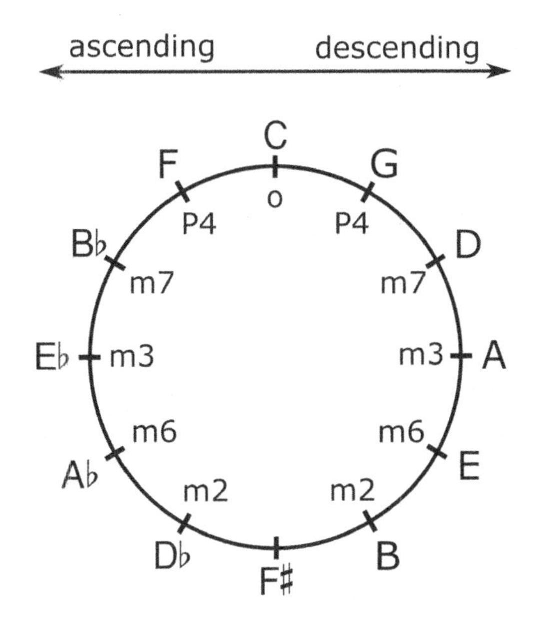


Figure 4.2: minor intervals & perfect 4th

Comparing figures 4.1 and 4.2, note the difference in the number of steps needed between a major interval and a minor interval of the same degree. For example, to move a major second up or down from a given note, you need to move two steps around the circle whereas for a minor second, you need to move five steps.

Again, comparing figures 4.1 and 4.2, you will see that the major second and the minor seventh are located at the same number of steps from the starting position but in opposite directions. This is because the major second and minor seventh are related by the one being the inversion of the other. So D is a major second up from C or a minor seventh down from C.

And of course, the same effect is seen for the other intervals :

- the perfect fourth is the inversion of the perfect fifth and vice-versa
- the major second is the inversion of the minor seventh and vice-versa
- the major third is the inversion of the minor sixth and vice-versa
- the major seventh is the inversion of the minor second and vice-versa
- the tritone is the inversion of the tritone

## The semitone

The semitone can be considered as a basic building block of intervals in our tempered system and is the smallest resolution available to us. This notion is sometimes scorned in more classical education but the semitone is more often referred to by jazz musicians who largely don't worry excessively about the difference between an augmented second and a minor third.

It is not a very practicable proposition to use the circle of fifths to envision semitone intervals but for those interested, a short discussion will be found in the appendix. [1]

## Intervals resource

A reasonably comprehensive cheat sheet of the simple intervals expressed in semitones is available for download. See the Resources section in Appendix E.

Exercise material on the contents of this chapter is available in *The Workbook: Volume 1 – Early Steps.*

1 See Appendix B, page 87

# 5 - The Relatives

There are several types of relationship between keys. We shall look at three of these: the major key's upper and lower relatives and its parallel minor. The circle of fifths can help you visualise them all more easily once you get used to the direction of travel for estimating minor thirds up and down.

## Moving a minor third round the circle

Keep in mind the convention we adopted for drawing the circle (see Chapter 1) ie with fifths ascending in a clockwise direction. Then we have minor thirds descending clockwise and ascending anti-clockwise. (Reminder : see Chapter 4)

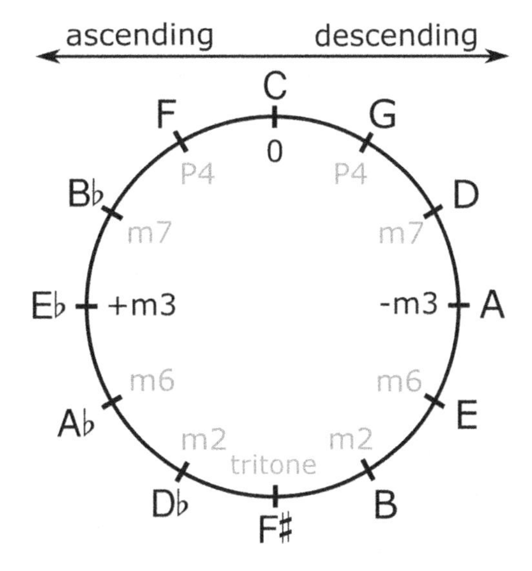


Figure 5.1: minors 3rds, up and down

Moving down a minor third from G arrives at E. Going up a minor third from F arrives at A♭. G to E represents a 90 degree segment of the circle (a quarter of its area).

## The relative minor

Each major key has a relative minor key sharing the same key signature. The relative minor is constructed on the sixth degree of the major scale and, in the case of the natural minor, uses the same set of pitches as the major.

The relative minor is the major key's lower relative. The tonics of the major scale and of its lower relative are separated by a minor third interval.

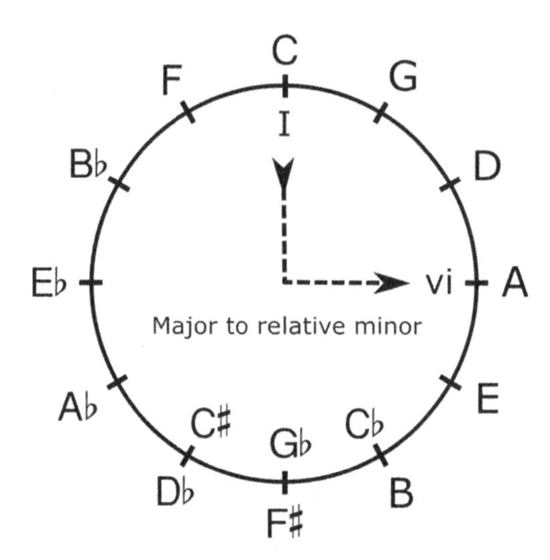


Figure 5.2: A is the relative minor key of C

C Major's relative minor is A minor and they share the same key signature which has neither flat nor sharp.

## The parallel pair

Each major scale also has a parallel minor scale. These two parallel scales are closely related because they share a common tonic note and the same dominant triad (in the harmonic and ascending melodic forms of the minor). Their key signatures are different.

The key signature of the parallel minor is the same as that of another major scale starting on its flattened third degree.

C Major's parallel minor is C minor. C minor's key signature is the same as E♭ Major's which has three flats.

## The upper relative

The upper relative of C minor is E♭ Major. Or looked at differently, E♭ Major's relative minor is C minor. See Figure 5.3.

Thus C Major has an upper relative, E♭ Major, thanks to its parallel minor, C minor.

The tonics of the major scale and of its upper relative are also a minor third apart.

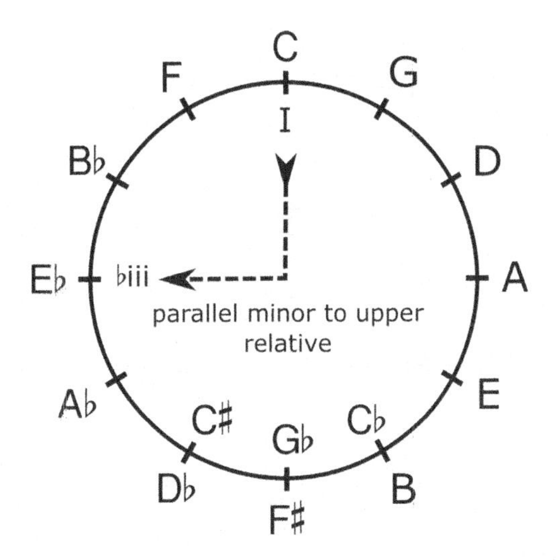


Figure 5.3: the upper relative

These relationships can be visualised easily with the circle of fifths now that we have seen how intervals of a minor third are shown on the circle. For any given tonic note, the minor third down is 90 degrees round the circle in the clockwise direction and the note's upper relative is 90 degrees round the circle in the anti-clockwise direction. 90 degrees represents the 3rd step around from the starting point.

Figure 5.4 shows the relative minor for C Major and the relative major for C minor.

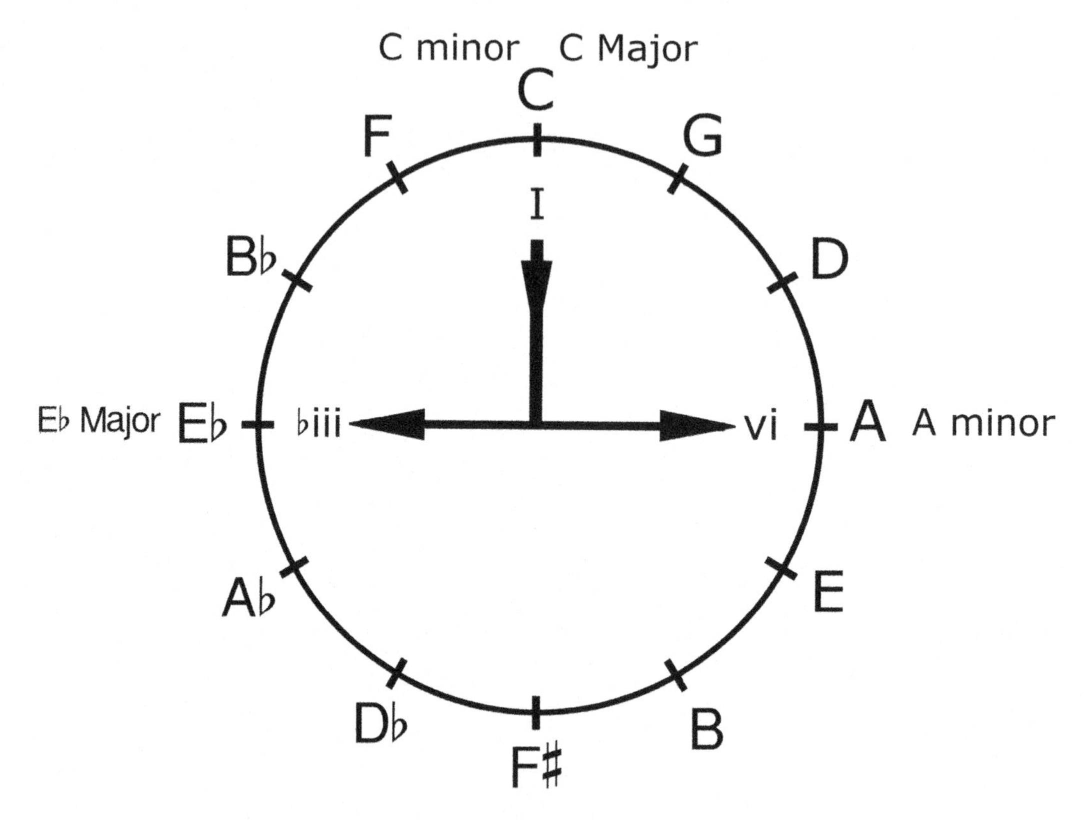


Figure 5.4: the relatives of C Major

- A minor is the relative minor of C Major.
- C minor is the parallel minor of C Major.
- E♭ Major is the upper relative of C minor.

Two further examples are given below.

Figure 5.5 shows the case with E as the tonic for the pair of parallel scales, E Major and E minor.

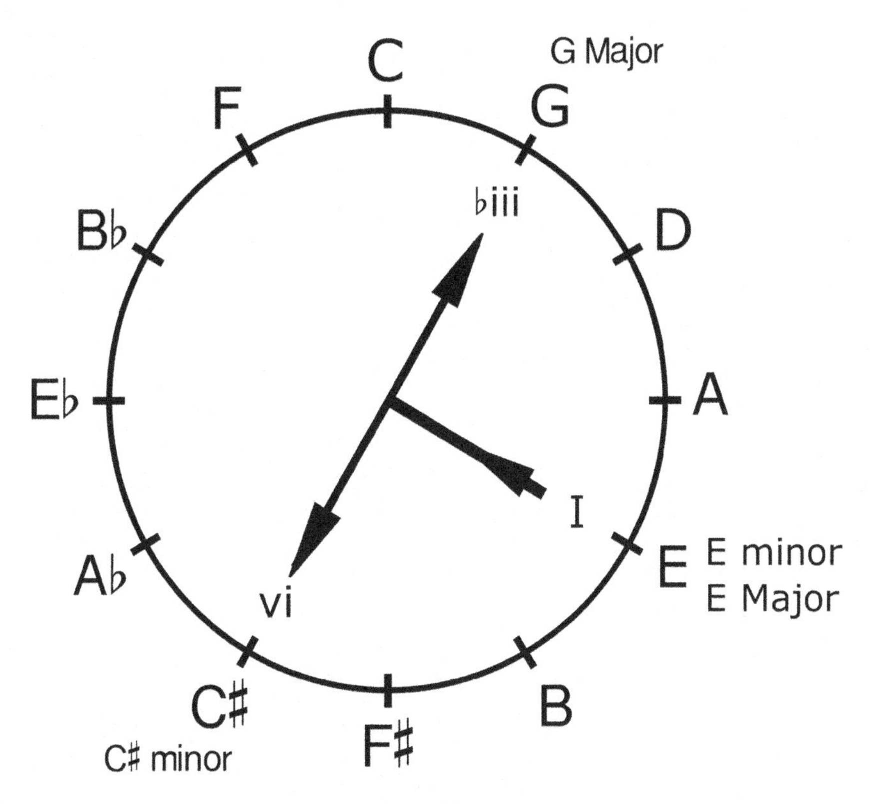


Figure 5.5: relatives of E Major

E Major has its parallel relative, E minor. E Major's relative minor is C♯ minor (not D♭ minor). E minor's relative major is G Major. As noted in Chapter 1, the appropriate spelling has to be selected for some of the members at the lower part of the circle.

Since we are dealing in this example with the relatives of E Major, a scale with 4 sharps in the key signature, it is appropriate to select C♯ minor with 7 sharps rather than D♭ minor which has 5 flats. That is for the theory but in practice, for performance, a musician may prefer to select the spelling with the fewer alterations in the key signature.

Figure 5.6 shows the case where A♭ is the tonic of A♭ Major and A♭ minor. F minor is the relative minor of A♭ Major and C♭ Major is the relative major of A♭ minor.

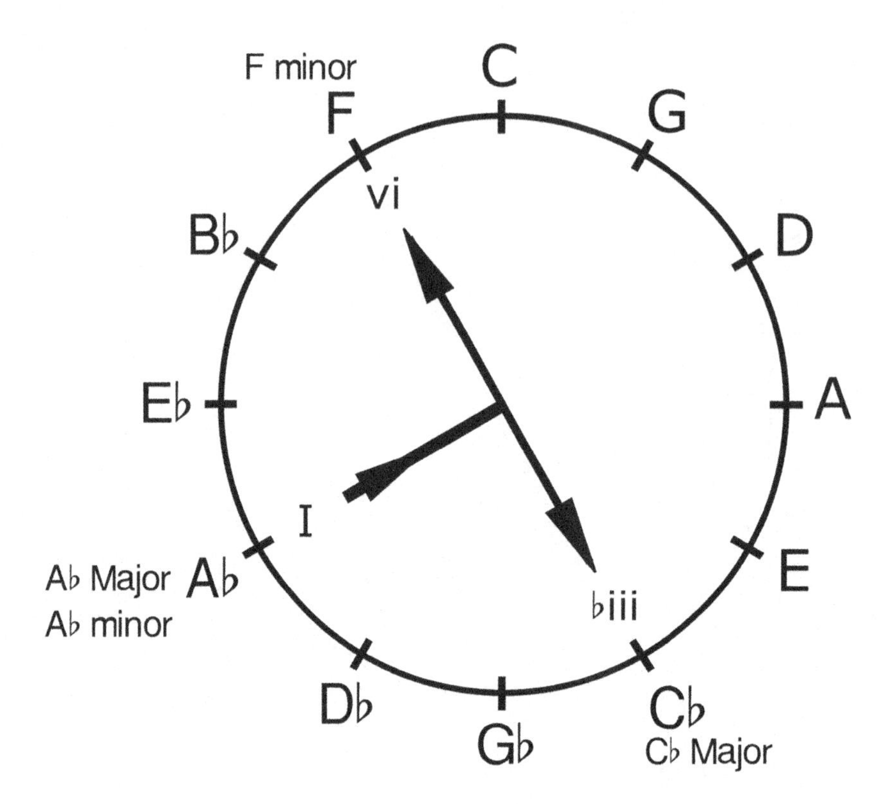


Figure 5.6: relatives of A♭ Major

A♭ Major has its parallel relative, A♭ minor. A♭ Major's relative minor is F minor. A♭ minor's relative major is C♭ Major. As noted in Chapter 1, the appropriate spelling has to be selected for some of the members at the lower part of the circle.

Exercise material on the contents of this chapter is available in *The Workbook: Volume 1 – Early Steps.*

# 6 - The Tritone

An interval of 3 tones or 6 semitones, the tritone is present in our major scales between the 4th and 7th degrees. It is also the equivalent of two successive minor third intervals. Our system of 12 semitones has six tritone intervals.

The tritone was referred to in the Middle Ages as the '*diabolus in musica*' and was detested because of its dissonance. Over the centuries, the human ear has become increasing accustomed to dissonance and the last interval waiting to be fully accepted is probably the minor second and even that interval finds its place today in some musical genres.

The tritone is considered the motor that propels the harmony onwards in jazz. Thus in the familiar ii – V7 – I progression, it is the tritone in the dominant seventh chord (between the 3rd and the 7th of the chord) which creates the instability indicating the need for resolution by the tonic chord.

Being able to recognise and form a tritone is a useful skill in improvised styles of music and this skill has its place establishing secondary dominants and diminished seventh chords. These will be covered in later chapters. For all of the above reasons, this is one of my favourite discoveries as a use for the circle of fifths.

The tritone interval is the sum of two consecutive minor thirds and we have seen in chapters 4 and 5 that the minor third is represented on the circle of fifths by a 90 degrees segment of the circle. Thus the tritone is represented by a straight line, a diameter.

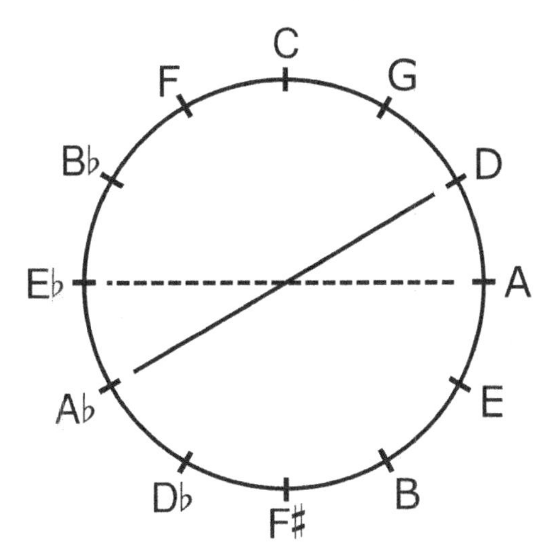


Figure 6.1: examples of the tritone interval

Two tritone intervals are shown in Figure 6.1 as examples : A – E♭ and D – A♭. The remaining four tritone intervals are : C – F♯ , G – D♭ , F – B, B♭ – E.

A tritone interval exists between the notes at either end of any diameter drawn on the circle of fifths.

Exercise material on the contents of this chapter is available in *The Workbook: Volume 1 – Early Steps.*

# 7 - Diminished and Augmented Chords

## Diminished chords

Another of my favourite uses for the circle of fifths is to visualise the components of a diminished seventh chord. This chord consists of a succession of four notes each a minor third apart and as such this chord is not diatonic to any major scale. In the minor scales, the diminished seventh chord only exists as a diatonic chord on the seventh degree of the harmonic minor. For example, in the scale of D♭ harmonic minor : on its seventh degree, C, we can construct Cdim7 which consists of C – E♭ – G♭ – B♭♭.

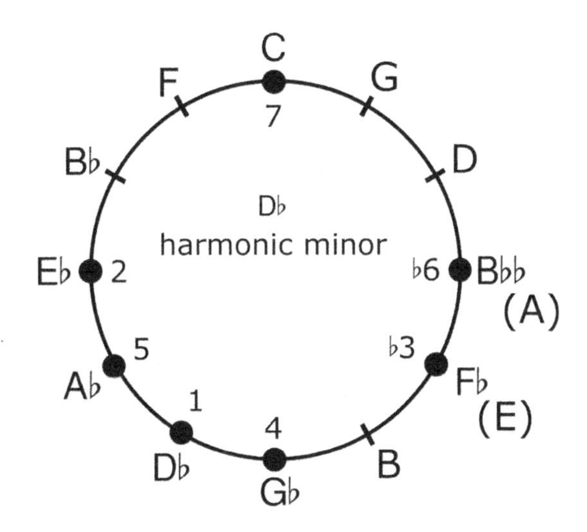


Figure 7.1: D♭ harmonic minor scale

The use of the double flat for B♭♭ will be avoided by many practising musicians who will respell this chord as C – E♭ – G♭ – A and thereby using an augmented second, G♭ – A to replace the minor third, G♭ – B♭♭, both intervals consisting of three semitones.

Such re-spelling is a very practical approach which will enable you to use the circle of fifths for a rapid assessment of the notes involved in any dim7 chord. It will not always be necessary to re-spell one of the notes every time.

You will remember from chapter 6 [1] that any diameter drawn on the circle represents a tritone interval and this is the equivalent of two successive minor thirds intervals. The dimin-

1 The tritone, page 23

ished seventh chord contains two tritone intervals and thus can be represented by two diameters as in the figure below. Because the chord is symmetrical, each interval being a minor third, the two diameters are at right angles.

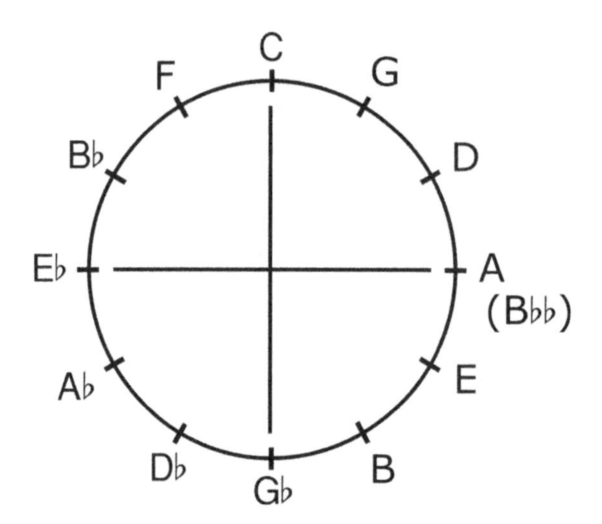


Figure 7.2: Cdim7 chord

Cdim7 consists of the four notes : C – E♭ – G♭ – A and the two tritones are C – G♭ and E♭ – A. Because this chord is symmetrical, all inversions of Cdim7 are also dim7 chords : E♭dim7, G♭dim7 and Adim7, which all contain the same set of notes (with enharmonic respelling as appropriate).

Let us look at the four cases where the dim7 chord is diatonic to a minor harmonic scale and constructed on its seventh degree..

- on vii of D♭ harmonic minor, Cdim7 : C – E♭ – G♭ – A
- on vii of F♭ harmonic minor, E♭dim7 : E♭ – G♭ – B♭♭ – D♭♭ which respells to E♭ – G♭ – A – C
- on vii of A♭♭ harmonic minor, G♭dim7 : Gb – B♭♭ – D♭♭ – F♭♭ which respells to G♭ – A – C – E♭
- on vii of B♭ harmonic minor, Adim7 : A – C – E♭ – G♭

These examples clearly show the practical interest of respelling to avoid double alterations.

There are only three different sets of notes which can be used to form diminished seventh chords.

- C – E♭ – G♭ – A
- G – B♭ – D♭ – E
- F – A♭ – B – D

These are shown in Figure 7.3 by the three different qualities of line.

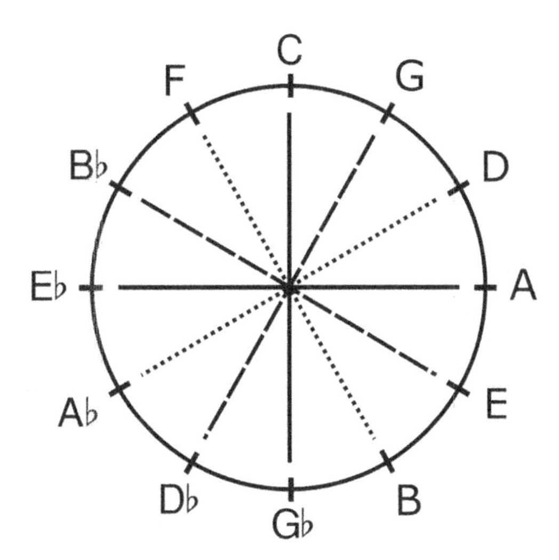


Figure 7.3: three families of dim7 chords

The three families of diminished seventh chords are :

Cdim7 (Cdim7, E♭dim7, G♭dim7, Adim7)

Gdim7 (Gdim7, B♭dim7, D♭dim7, Edim7)

Fdim7 (Fdim7, A♭dim7, Bdim7, Ddim7)

## As a rootless ninth chord

Frequently associated with diminished seventh chords are seventh chords with a ♭9. Look closely at the examples below :

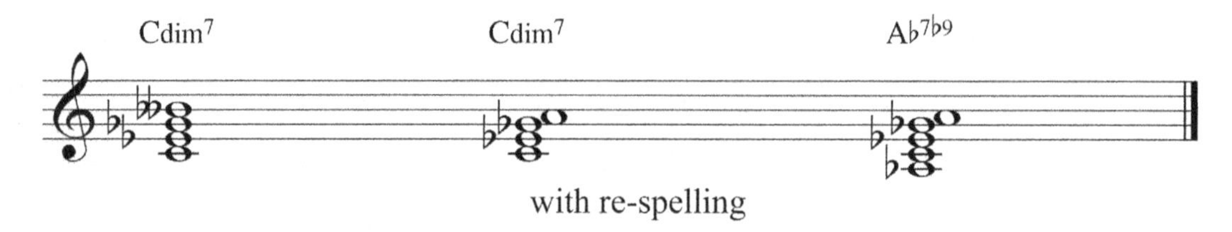


Figure 7.4: Cdim7 as upper structure of A♭7♭9 chord

Cdim7 is none other than A♭7♭9 without the bass note. Both chords are diatonic to the harmonic minor scale : the dim7 on the vii degree and the 7♭9 on the V degree.

This brings me to the next requirement which frequently is to convert the dim7 chord into a corresponding 7♭9 chord. For that, it suffices to find the note which is a major third below any of the diminished seventh notes.

To find a major third below any given note is very easy to visualise on the circle. We have already seen this in Chapter 4. [2] From that given note, take 4 steps to the left. See figure 7.5 below.

This will give four possible bass notes. In the case of our Cdim7, these will be :

- A♭ (a major third below C)
- B (a major third below E♭)
- D (a major third below F♯ or G♭)
- F (a major third below A)

You will notice that these in turn form another diminished seventh chord :

A♭ – B – D – F

Figure 7.5 shows this new dim7 chord together with the original.

2 Major third descending, page 14

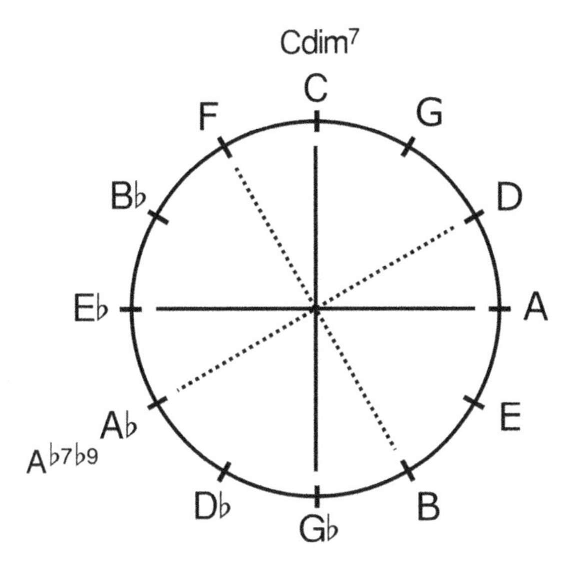


Figure 7.5: A♭$^{7\flat 9}$ with upper structure Cdim7

Which note you select will naturally depend on the musical context but for our purposes with the circle, note that the four possibilities involve another diminished seventh chord displaced one step round to the left from our original diminished seventh chord.

## Augmented chords

The augmented triad is formed of two superposed major thirds and so it divides the octave into three equal parts. Like the diminished chord, the augmented chord is symmetrical so the first and second inversion do not change the quality of the sound.

Take as an example, the C augmented triad : C – E – G♯. Major thirds increase in the clock-wise sense. On our circle, we shall have to keep in mind the various enharmonic spellings.

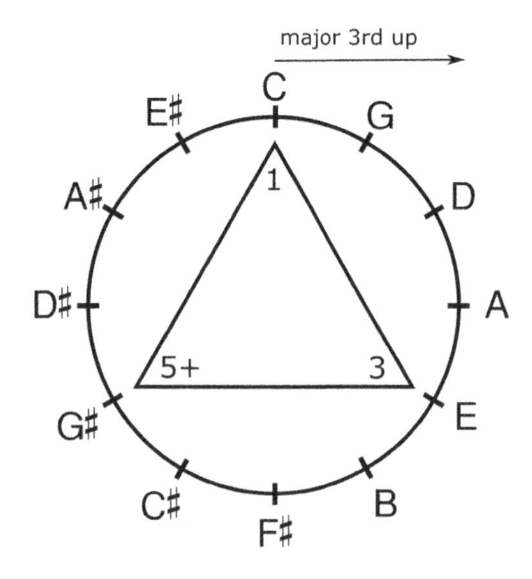


Figure 7.6: Caug triad

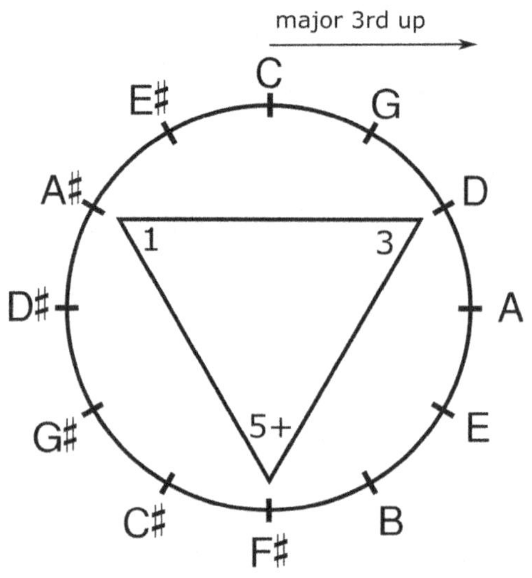

Figure 7.7: Daug triad

There are therefore only four sets of notes to form augmented triad chords. The four families of augmented triads are :

- Caug (Caug, Eaug, G♯aug)
- Gaug (Gaug, Baug, D♯aug)
- Daug (Daug, F♯aug, A♯aug)
- Aaug (Aaug, C♯aug, E♯aug)

A group of two augmented chords, Caug + Daug, taken together, forms the six notes of the C whole tone scale.

Similarly, Gaug + Aaug form the six notes of the other whole note scale, conventionally known as the C♯ whole tone scale. [3]

Exercise material on the contents of this chapter is available in *The Workbook: Volume 1 – Early Steps.*

3 For further remarks on the whole tone scale see Chapter 10.

# 8 - Substitute Dominants

The use of diatonic progressions in descending fifths is frequently used, especially in jazz. It provides linear progressions of chordal 3rds and 7ths as shown in this example :

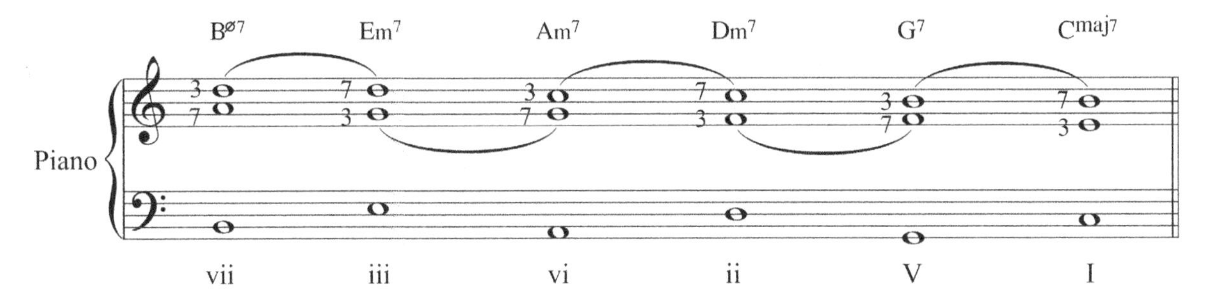


Figure 8.1: Typical succession of 3rds and 7ths in progression by descending fifths

Such a diatonic descent, if used too frequently, can become a little monotonous with its succession of minor chords from the iii, vi, ii degrees of the major scale. To reduce the predictability, we can substitute secondary dominants in some cases and use tritone substitution to provide a chromatic dominant in others.

## Tritone substitution

If we look at a standard ii – V7 – I progression, in the key of C Major this is Dm7 – G7 – Cmaj7. To apply tritone substitution to the G dominant seven chord, we need to select another dominant chord containing the same tritone. The tritone in a dominant seventh chord is formed between the 3rd and the 7th of the chord. For G7 this is between the notes B and F.

Here comes the exciting part played by the circle of fifths diagram. In Chapter 6 we showed that the notes at either end of a diameter across the circle of fifths form a tritone interval (see Figure 6.1). The other point of interest to us is that dominant seventh chords formed on these two notes, a tritone apart, contain the same tritone between their 3$^{rd}$ and their 7$^{th}$.

Again, using the key of C Major, the dominant seventh G7, constructed with its root as G, consists of the notes G - B - D - F. The third is B and the seventh is F : they are diametrically opposed on the circle and they are a tritone apart.

Look at the circle in Figure 8.2 and move from G across the circle on its diameter and we arrive at D♭. Building a dominant seventh chord on the root of D♭, gives D♭ - F - A♭ - C♭. If we respell the seventh as B instead of C♭, we find D♭7 has the same tritone, F and B, as G7, albeit inverted. A tritone interval inverted remains a tritone interval.

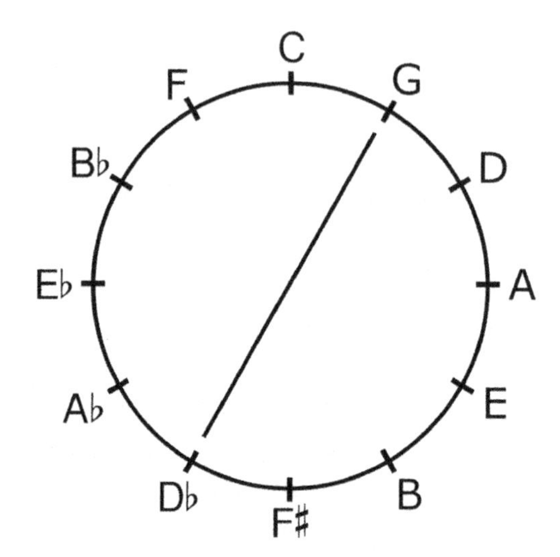


Figure 8.2: roots separated by a tritone

**Two dominant seventh chords whose roots are a tritone apart will each contain the same tritone between their 3rd and their 7th.**

## Substitute or chromatic dominants

Our original ii – V – I progression, Dm7 – G7 – Cmaj7, can now become Dm7 – D♭7 – Cmaj7, ie ii – ♭ii – I, while retaining its same character because the tritone in the dominant seventh is unchanged.

The easy visualisation permitted by our use of the circle of fifths is demonstrated in Figure 8.3 below.

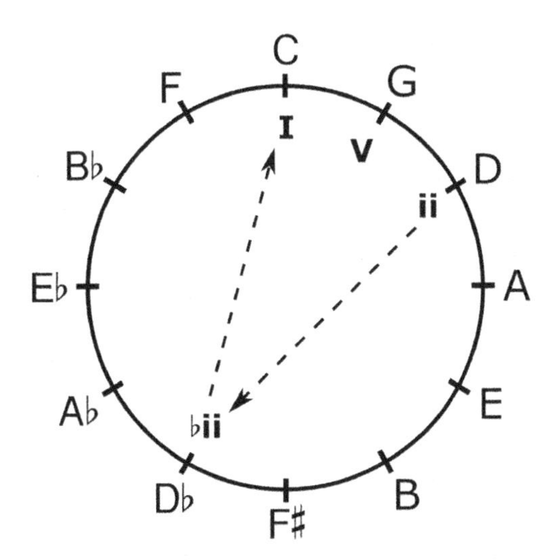


Figure 8.3: D♭7 substitutes for G7

The root movement changes from a descent of fifths, D – G – C, to a chromatic descent D – D♭ – C. This technique is frequently exploited by bass players.

A chromatic ascent of the root is also seen quite frequently and is often of this type :

I maj7 – ♯I dim7 – ii m7

This progression was mentioned earlier in Chapter 7. [1]

1 Rootless ninth chords, page 28

## Bartok substitutions

During the development of music towards a more free use of all the twelve notes of the chromatic scale in the late 19th and early 20th centuries, the composer Bela Bartok extended the notion of tonic, sub-dominant and dominant functions first to the secondary minor triads and then to all twelve notes.

The vi degree was associated with the tonic function, the ii degree with the sub-dominant function and the iii degree with the dominant function. Each of these three secondary degrees was a minor third below its associated primary degree ( ii – IV, iii – V, vi – I ). By extension, the vii degree was associated with ii degree, ♭V – vi, ♭ii – iii, ♭vi – vii, ♭iii – ♭V, ♭vii – ♭ii. All twelve notes of the chromatic scale were associated with either the tonic (T), the sub-dominant (SD) or the dominant (D) function as shown in the Figure below.

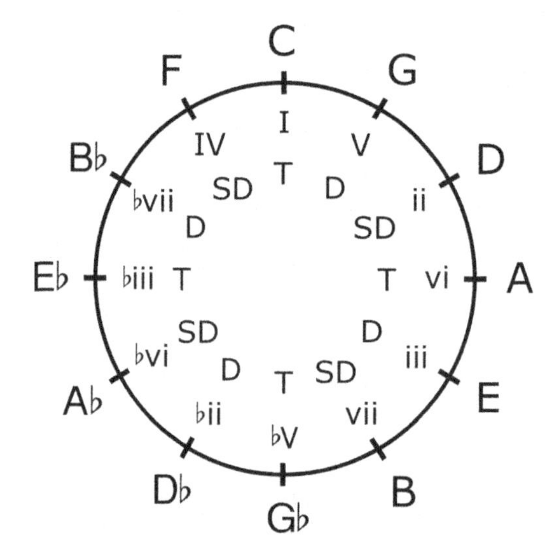


Figure 8.4: functions on degrees of C Major

For any given function, say the dominant, Bartok had a primary axis going from the V degree straight across the circle of fifths to ♭ii (a distance of a tritone from the V degree) and a secondary axis crossing the primary axis at right angles. This secondary axis, in the case of the dominant function, ran from the ♭vii to the iii degree. Thus each function is associated with four degrees equally spaced around the circle in intervals of a minor third.

Although we are looking at functionally related tonalities and the four notes do not form a chord but are only functionally related, in practical terms we can think about them on the circle as we would a diminished seventh chord. This presumption makes it easier for us to visualise the four alternatives for substitution.

In the case of C Major, the V degree is G, the ♭ii is D♭, the ♭vii is B♭ and the iii degree is E. These four notes form four poles of dominant function and we can imagine them as a diminished seventh chord, Gdim7. For more on diminished chords, see Chapter 7, page 25.

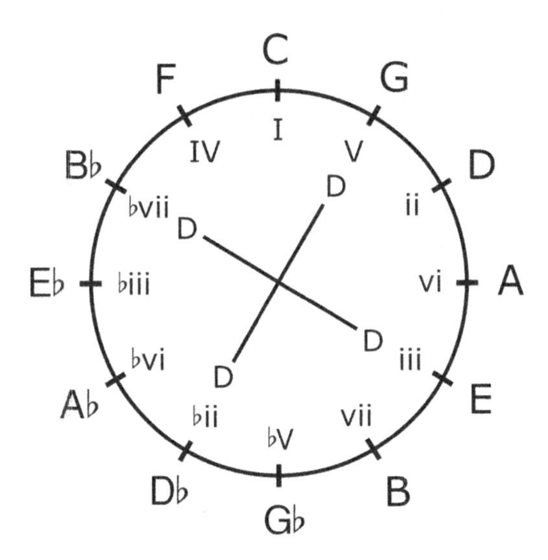


Figure 8.5: Bartok substitutes in C Major

Because there is this functional equivalence between the four notes, one can be substituted for the other. We have already seen the tritone substitution of dominants. [2] The two roots concerned, V and ♭ii, are those represented by the primary axis in Bartok's work. The other two roots, ♭vii and iii, on the secondary axis, can also be used.

A ii – V – I progression, Dm7 – G7 – Cmaj7 can become :

- ii – ♭ii – I : Dm7 – D♭7 – Cmaj7 (a standard tritone substitution)
- ii – ♭vii – I : Dm7 – B♭7 – Cmaj7
- ii – iii – I : Dm7 – E7 – Cmaj7 This latter is seen less often.

2 page 33

Just as G7 and D♭7 share the same tritone, B – F, so B♭7 and E7 share the same tritone, D – A♭.

Exercise material on the contents of this chapter is available in *The Workbook: Volume 2 – Further Steps.*

# 9 - Chord Progressions

In many musical genres, an understanding of the chord progressions which make up the harmonisation of the melody is useful. A preliminary phase to understanding a new piece of music is to make an analysis of the harmony which may be informal or more detailed. Where improvisation is concerned, an understanding of the basis of the chord progressions is vital to the realisation of a good performance.

The circle of fifths provides a useful tool for both a rapid and a more detailed appreciation of the harmonic progressions. Once the circle is committed to memory, the different chord progressions can be seen in the mind's eye.

Common progressions are : the cadences IV – I ; ii – V – I ; the turnarounds vi – ii – V – I and iii – vi – ii – V – I. These are based on the principle that the root note descends a fifth (or rises a fourth) with the passage from one chord to another. Such a movement is considered strong in music theory.

Look first at Figure 9.1 which shows the diatonic degrees of a major scale in bold.

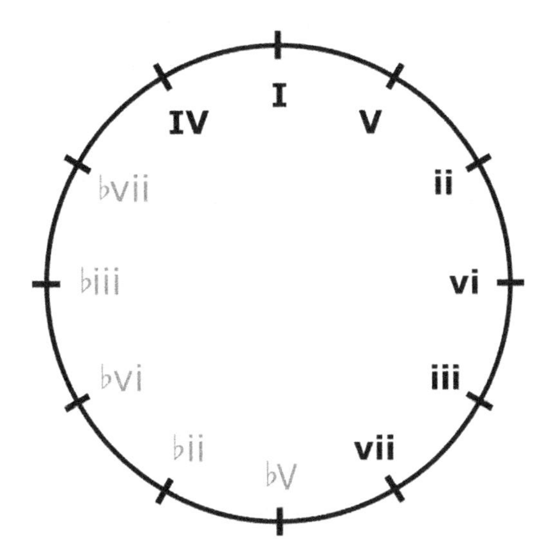


Figure 9.1: Scale degrees

Note carefully the positions of degrees IV, V, ii, vi, iii.

Now compare the following examples in Figure 9.2 :

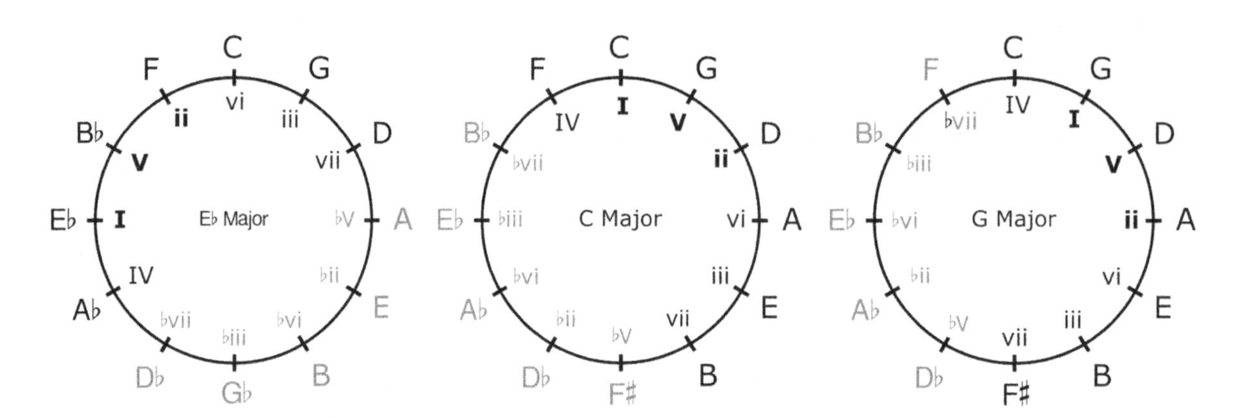


Figure 9.2: ii-V-I highlighted in E♭ Major, C Major and G Major

They are always in this same relative position with respect to the tonic, I. This makes it easy for us to visualise progressions in fourths and fifths.

## Secondary dominants

The first thing to notice is the V – I part of the ii – V – I progression. Because the circle is based on intervals of a fifth, every step anti-clockwise involves the descent of a fifth. Any time we wish to proceed from say, E to A we can do so by creating a dominant seventh on the E and then moving one step round to resolve on A.

If this move is only part of a longer series of moves, we do not need to go from E7 to Amaj7 but can go from E7 to A7 to D7 … and further. These are secondary dominants and are of course not diatonic to the current key.

Any dominant seventh can be preceded by its minor seventh to form a cadence of ii – V – I which will tend to confirm the tonality of the key of I.

## The ii – V – I progression

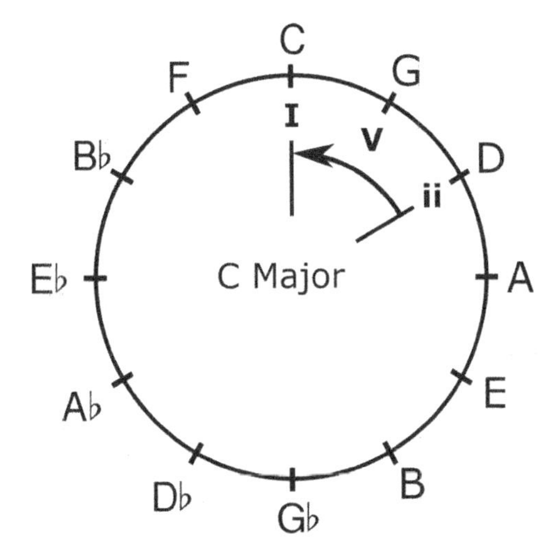


Figure 9.3: ii – V – I progression to C Major

For any given tonic note, I, the ii – V – I progression starts two steps round the circle in the clockwise direction from the tonic. This is the position of the ii chord. The progression then moves one step anti-clockwise to the V chord and again one more step to the tonic.

## Major keys

With major scales, the ii is a minor seventh chord, the V7 is a dominant seventh and the I is a major seventh. Figure 9.3 shows, in the key of C Major, the ii – V – I progression of Dm7 – G7 – Cmaj7.

Figure 9.4 shows three further examples, below.

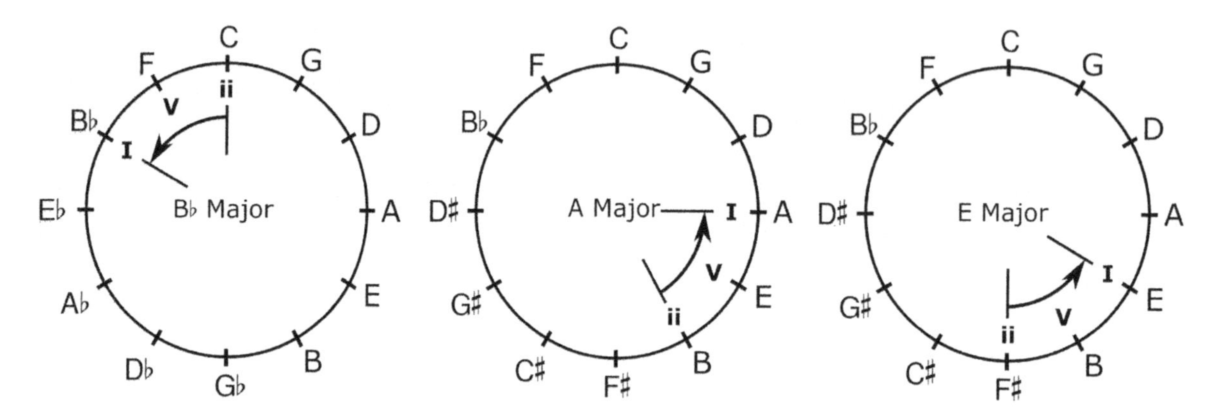


Figure 9.4: three ii – V – I progressions in these keys : B♭ Major, A Major, E Major

Figure 9.4 shows the same pattern in three keys, always moving two steps clockwise :

- in B♭ Major : Cm7 – F7 – B♭maj7
- in A Major : Bm7 – E7 – Amaj7
- in E Major : F♯m7 – B7 – Emaj7

## Minor keys

The harmonisation of minor scales is more rich and varies according to whether we have natural minor, harmonic minor or melodic minor. We will take for our examples the case of the harmonic minor variants.

In the harmonic minor scales, the second degree is iiø (or half-diminished), the fifth degree is V7♭9, and the first degree is minor with major seventh : iiø - V7♭9 – i m.maj7.

We can take the keys of Figure 9.4. as minor. This shows the same pattern in three keys, always jumping two steps clockwise from the scale tonic to the second degree and then returning step by step :

- in B♭ minor : CØ – F7♭9 – B♭m.maj7
- in A minor : BØ – E7♭9 – Am.maj7
- in E minor : F♯Ø – B7♭9 – Em.maj7

# The vi – ii – V – I and iii – vi – ii – V – I progressions

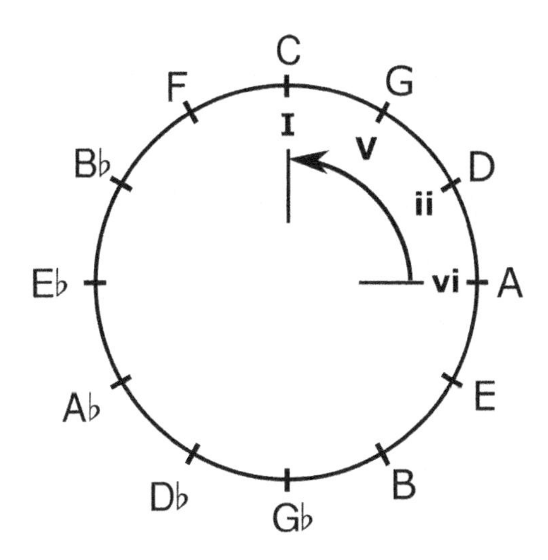


Figure 9.5: vi – ii – V – I progression in C Major

We have seen how the ii – V – I progression always moves the same way regardless of the key. The vi – ii – V – I works the same way but with a starting point one further step round to the right.

Figure 9.5 shows the progression from Am7 through Dm7 and G7 to Cmaj7. If the sequence starts one further step round to the right, we have the iii – vi – ii – V – I progression.

The vi degree is sometimes taken as a secondary dominant V7/ii, A7, instead of a diatonic Am7. This secondary dominant may be preceded by its own ii to give a progression Em7 – A7 – Dm7 – G7 – Cmaj7. In all these cases, the principle is the same for each key.

Further examples are shown below, in Figure 9.6 :

- On the left, a iii – vi – ii – V – I diatonic progression of Dm7 – Gm7 – Cm7 – F7 – B♭ Major.
- In the centre, a vi – ii – V – I diatonic progression of F♯m7 – Bm7 – E7 – to A Major.
- On the right, a iii – vi – ii – V – I diatonic progression of Em7 – Am7 – Dm7 – G7 – to C Major.

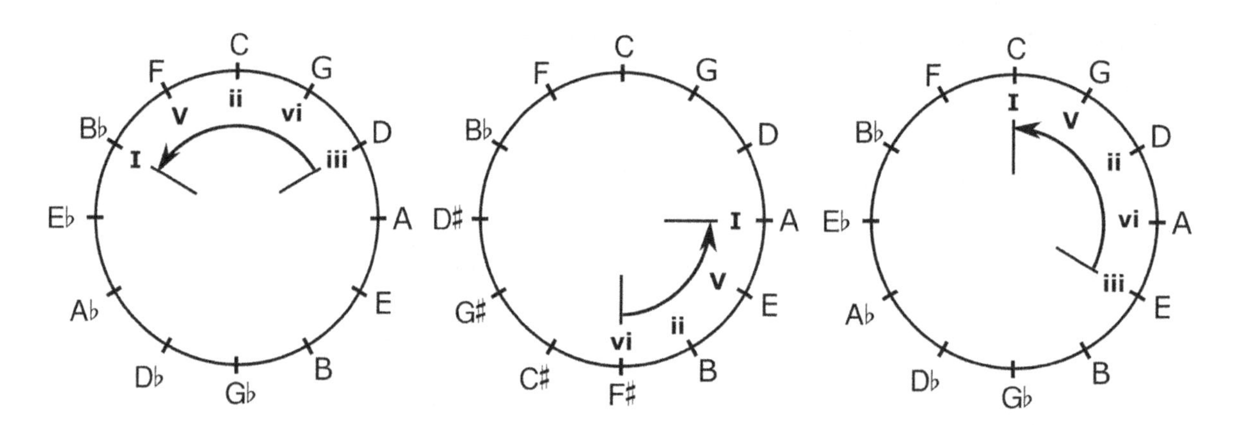


Figure 9.6: examples of progressions to B♭ Major, to A Major and to C Major

## The diatonic progression through the full octave

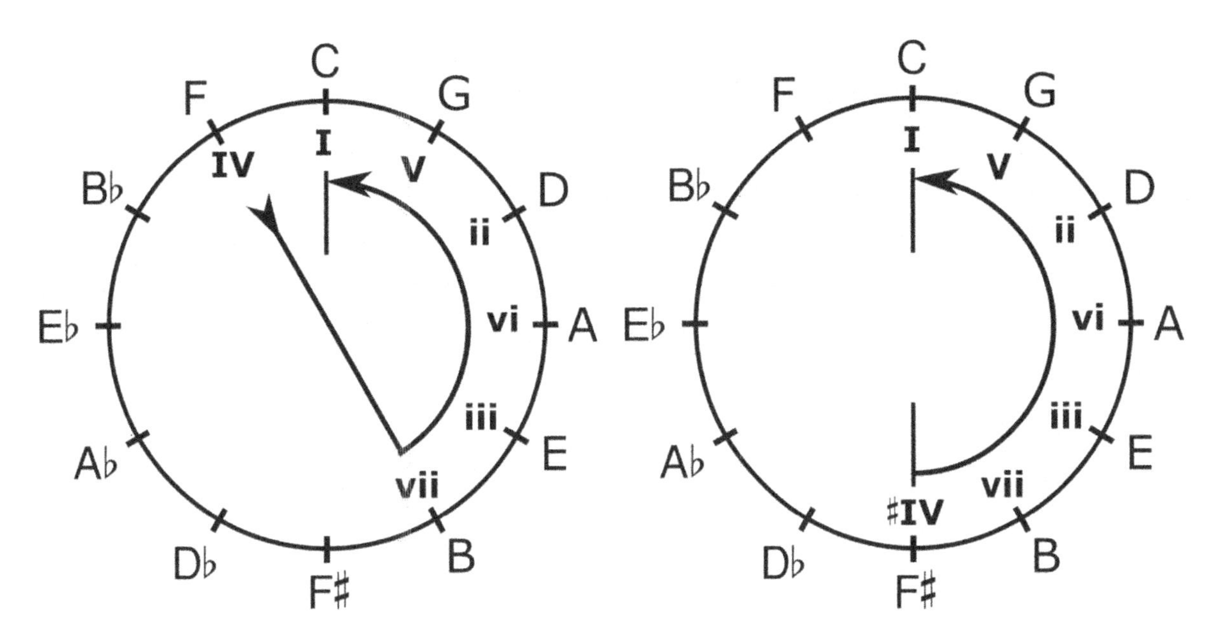


Figure 9.7: Full diatonic progression in C Major, on left, with alternative starting at ♯IV

The difficulty with a diatonic progression through the full octave, IV – viiø – iii – vi – ii – V7 – I, is that the movement of the bass from IV – viiø is not a perfect fifth but a tritone. To avoid the tritone, the Lydian fourth is often inserted in place of the fourth i.e. ♯IV instead of IV.

In C Major this would mean replacing :

Fmaj7 – Bø – Em7 – Am7 – Dm7 – G7 – Cmaj7

by

F♯maj7 – Bø – Em7 – Am7 – Dm7 – G7 – Cmaj7

# Chromatic progressions

For various aesthetic reasons, musicians will prefer from time to time to chose a chromatic progression either with roots ascending or descending.

## descending chromatic progression

A primary tool for preparing a chromatically descending root progression is by tritone substitution of the ♭ii chord for the dominant V chord in, say, a standard ii – V – I progression. The basics of tritone substitution have been covered in Chapter 8. [1]

By this means, we replace a ii – V – I progression with ii – ♭ii – I progression but we do not need to stop there. The principle can be applied to a longer series of secondary dominants by crossing and recrossing the circle.

For example, in Figure 9.8 below, a series like B7 – E7 – A7 – Dm7 – G7 – Cmaj7 could be changed to the following chromatically descending progression : F7 – E7 – E♭7 – Dm7 – D♭7 – Cmaj7.

F and B, A and E♭, G and D♭ are three pairs of notes at opposite ends of diameters on the circle and therefore each pair forms the interval of a tritone.

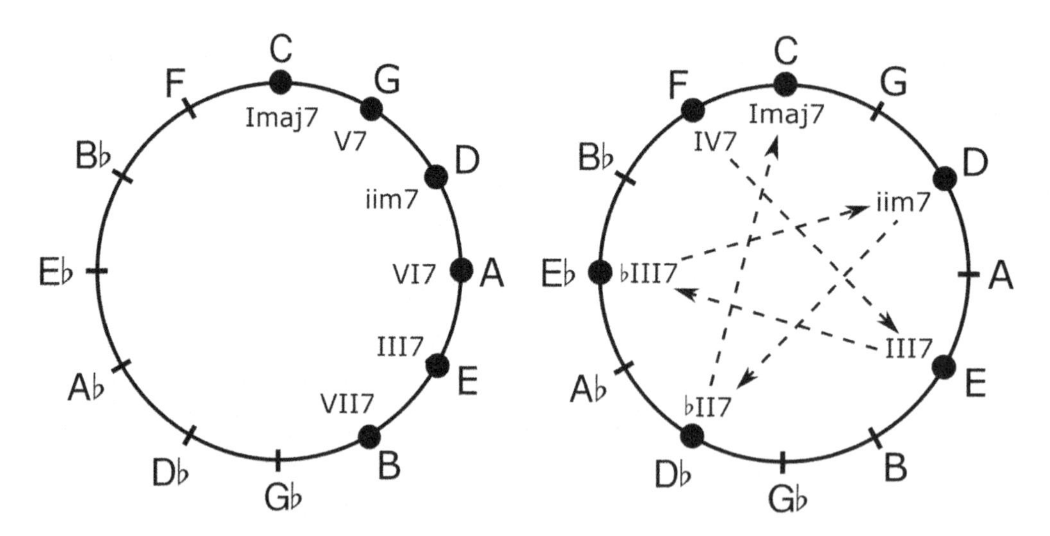


Figure 9.8: descent by fifths becomes chromatic descent by tritone substitution

1 Tritone substitution, page 31

## ascending chromatic progression

Musicians often come across progressions ascending chromatically of the type I – ♯I – ii – V – I. The star player in these cases is the diminished seventh chord which can resolve in so many different ways that it can be used as an approach chord, a passing chord as well as being used in a dominant function.

A rootless dominant finds a use as a substitute dominant in a chromatic ascent of the type Imaj7 – ♯Idim7 – iim7. A standard I – ii – V – I progression can be extended by inserting the V/ii chord. Since the ii is a minor seventh chord, we may borrow its dominant from the related harmonic minor scale having ii as its tonic. The V of a harmonic minor scale is of the type V7♭9 and we can discard its root and use the upper structure only which is a dim7 chord. [2]

Taking C Major as an example : the I – ii – V – I progression is Cmaj7 – Dm7 – G7 – Cmaj7. V/ii in this case means borrowing a chord from D harmonic minor from which we use the V chord, A7♭9 ie A C♯ - E - G - B♭ and this is C♯dim7 on a root of A (C♯dim7/A). Because the dim7 chord also contains the same tritone as the V7, it can act as a dominant to the ii.

The result is that our progression now becomes : Imaj7 – ♯Idim7 – iim7 – V7 – Imaj7 or for C Major : Cmaj7 – C♯dim7 – Dm7 – G7 – Cmaj7

Similar reasoning will enable this progression to be extended :

Imaj7 – ♯Idim7 – iim7 – ♯iidim7 – iiim7 etc

or

Cmaj7 – C♯dim7 – Dm7 – D♯dim7 – Em7

2 Rootless ninth chords, Chapter 7, page 28

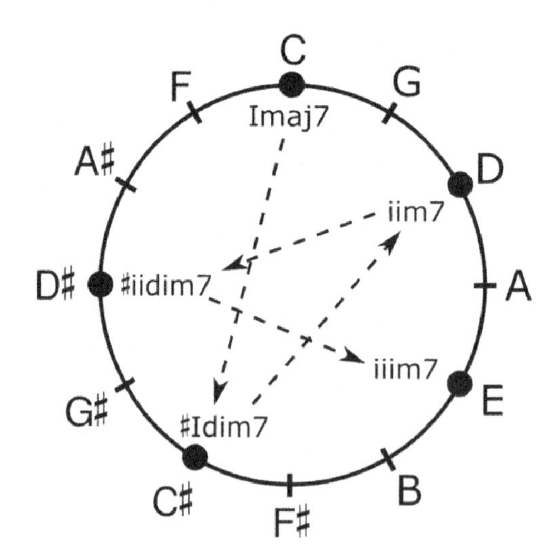


Figure 9.9: chromatic ascending progression

Although figure 9.9 resembles somewhat the previous figure, here it is not a matter of tri-tone substitution but rather an example of one of the possible resolutions of the dim7 chord. In this case, the dim7 chord is resolved by 2 notes rising a semitone and the other 2 rising a full tone to turn the dim7 into a m7 chord with its root a semitone higher.

## The basic blues progression

A very basic version of the twelve bar blues is the following progression using the key of F as an illustration :

| F7 (I) | F7 (I) | F7 (I) | F7 (I) |
|---|---|---|---|
| B♭7 (IV) | B♭7 (IV) | F7 (I) | F7 (I) |
| C7 (V) | B♭7 (IV) | F7 (I) | F7 (I) |

This progression uses three adjacent members on the circle. First, the I7 chord for four bars and then followed by a single step to the left to the IV7 chord for two bars before moving back one step right to the I7 chord. The eighth bar requires another step to the right to the V7 chord followed by two steps to the left to the IV7 chord and then one step again to the right to the I7 chord.

There are multiple versions of this grid many becoming quite complex but the basic grid uses dominant chords and the only one that is truly diatonic to the scale is the V7.

What interests us is the fact that everything happens using three adjacent elements in the circle of fifths : I and its two neighbors : IV to the left and V to the right. The whole of the basic 12 bars grid consists of a to and fro movement from I to IV and back to I and then to V and IV and finally completes with a move back to I to start the second cycle.

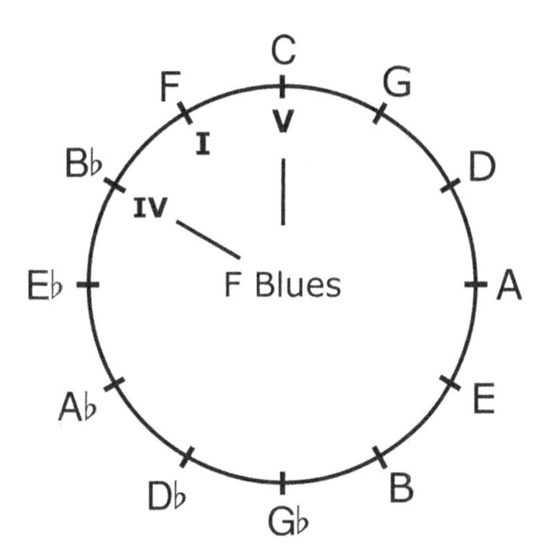


Figure 9.10: Blues in F

In F Blues :

- the I7 is F7 and this is diatonic to the key of B♭ major
- the IV7 is B♭7 and this is diatonic to the key of E♭ major
- the V7 is C7 and this is the one which is diatonic to the the key of F major.

Common Blues practice would be to associate this progression with the Blues scale or the three Mixolydian modes : F Mixolydian, B♭ Mixolydian, C Mixolydian.

Exercise material on the contents of this chapter is available in *The Workbook: Volume 2 – Further Steps.*

Notes

# 10 - Whole tone and other scales

## The whole tone scale

This is a scale consisting of six different note names. It is a fine candidate for being illustrated on a circle because of its symmetry. You can see quite clearly that only two different scales can be defined within the twelve notes existing in our tempered tonal system. The notes in each scale are separated by a semitone and conventionally are named as 'C whole tone' and 'D♭ (C♯) whole tone'. Starting on any other note will only give another mode of one of these two scales.

In Figure 10.1 below, we show the two possibilities :

C whole tone scale : C D E F♯ G♯ A♯
D♭ whole tone scale : D♭ E♭ F G A B

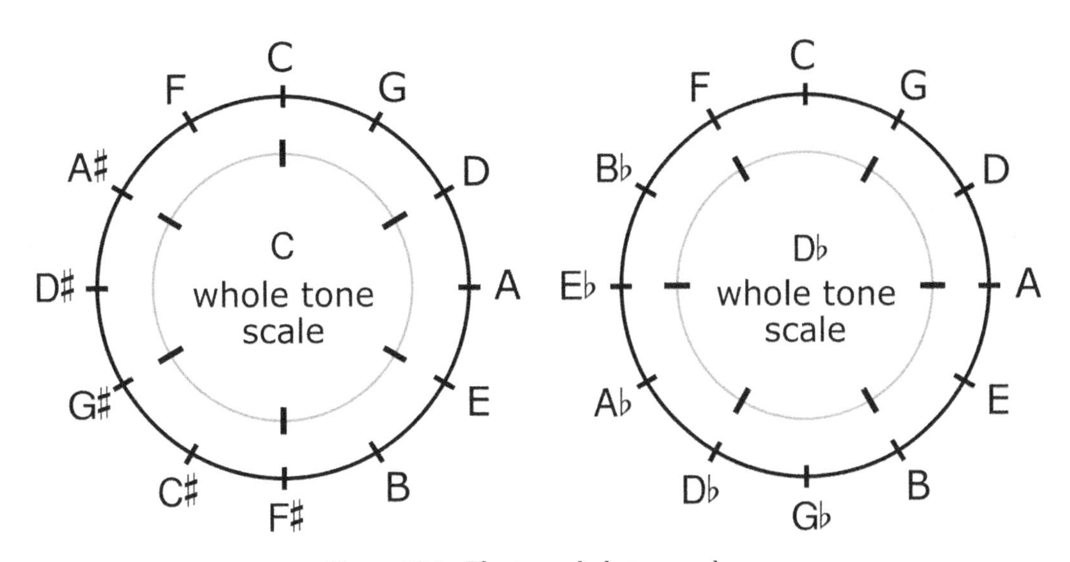


Figure 10.1: The two whole tone scales

The whole tone scale is intimately related to the augmented triad. [1] Harmonisation of the whole tone scale gives only augmented triads and furthermore, this scale can be considered to be made of two interlaced augmented triads : C - E - G♯ and D - F♯ - A♯. This can easily be visualised on the circle as we show below in Figure 10.2.

1 See Chapter 7, page 29

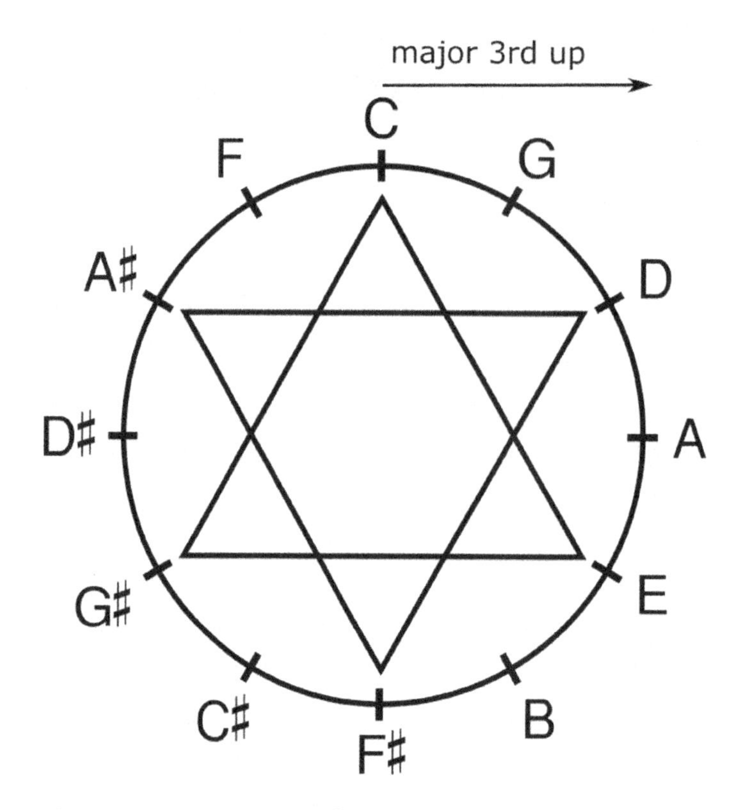


Figure 10.2: two augmented triads forming a whole tone scale

This scale contains three tritones : C – F♯ (G♭), D – G♯ (A♭), E – A♯ (B♭). As we have seen earlier (chapter 6), the instability of this interval assists in transformation to other chords or tonalities. The whole tone scale finds many uses in modulations.

One example is the use of complex chords in quartal harmony. For example, a six member quartal chord such as B - E - A - D - G - C can evolve by lowering three members by a semitone to provide another chord : A♯ - E - G♯ - D - F♯ - C. You will see immediately that these are the six notes named at the beginning of this chapter as the C whole tone scale although they are in a different order. [2]

2 See Chapter 12, page 75

# The diminished scale

The diminished scale is octotonic and symmetric in that it is formed of alternating steps of whole tones and half tones. Hence it is closely related to the diminished seventh chord. In fact, looking at the scale plotted on the circle, it is formed of the notes of two diminished seven chords.

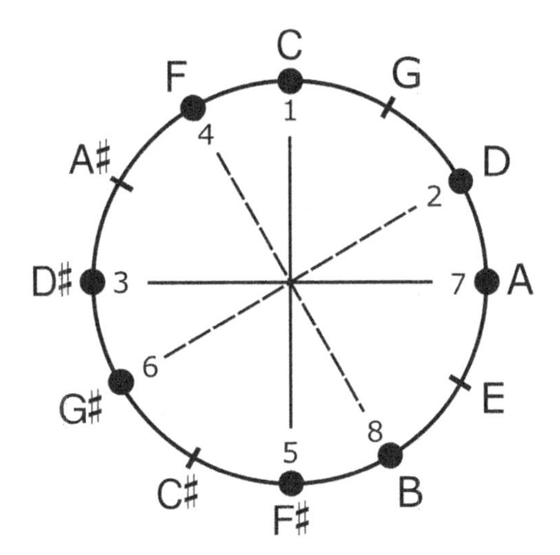


Figure 10.3: C diminished T-½ scale

From figure 10.3, you can see that the order of plotting is from degree 1, two steps to the right (up one tone) for degree 2 followed by five steps to the left (up one semitone) for degree 3. This sequence is repeated until all 8 notes are drawn. In effect, the odd numbered degrees form a first diminished seven chord (the solid lined cross) and the even numbered degrees form a second diminished chord (the dashed cross).

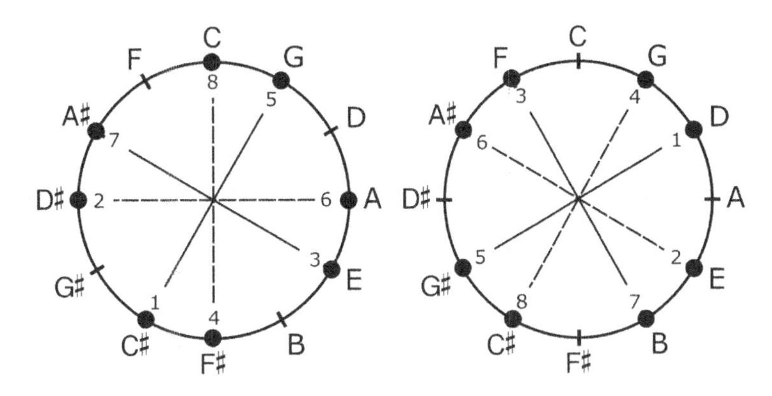


Figure 10.4: T-½ octotonic scales in C♯ and D

There are only three distinct versions of the diminished T – ½ scale and these are conventionally named as C, C♯ and D. Figures 10.3 and 10.4 show all three of these scales :

- C D D♯ F F♯ G♯ A B
- C♯ D♯ E F♯ G A A♯ C
- D E F G G♯ A♯ B C♯

They form a pattern which is easy to visualise on the circle. First visualise a diminished seventh chord on the tonic of the corresponding major scale and then add another diminished chord on the IV degree of the major scale.

Try this example of determining the eight notes in the tone - semitone diminished scale in F. The four notes of the diminished seventh chord on I are : F, G♯, B, D and the four notes of the diminished chord on IV are : B♭, D♭, E, G. Combined, these give : F G G♯ B♭ B D♭ D E. With enharmonic respelling to avoid mixing flats and sharps, we have the

F w-½ diminished scale : F G G♯ A♯ B C♯ D E

You can see straight away that this scale is a mode of the D T-½ diminished scale. So there is little incentive to construct any other than the three basic forms.

The improvising musician will probably not be concerned unduly with having these notes in scale order nor necessarily too worried about mixing sharps and flats.

## The inverted diminished scale

The other version of the diminished scale is an alternation of semitones and tones. The ½-T is often referred to as inverted diminished or simply diminished. In any case, the set of notes in each of three possible scales is identical to those in one of the three T-½ diminished scales.

The ½-T diminished is a mode of the T-½ diminished scale.

# The diminished whole tone scale

The diminished whole tone scale is so called because it starts out like a diminished scale with a series of two semitone – tone sequences and finishes off to complete its seven note complement with a series of whole tones.

It goes under several alternative names like the Superlocrian mode or the altered scale but in fact, it is the seventh mode of the melodic minor scale.

To illustrate this scale, consider the C diminished whole tone scale :

C D♭ E♭ F♭ G♭ A♭ B♭ C  a series of intervals : ½ – T – ½ – T – T – T – T

You could remember that this is the 7th mode of D♭ melodic minor scale but probably the simplest way to generate this scale is to think Superlocrian and take the major scale on the same tonic, C Major, keep the tonic unchanged and flatten all the other six notes. For a melodic analysis :

1 ♭2 ♭3 ♭4 ♭5 ♭6 ♭7

This scale is not a beauty to remember on the circle, figure 10.5.

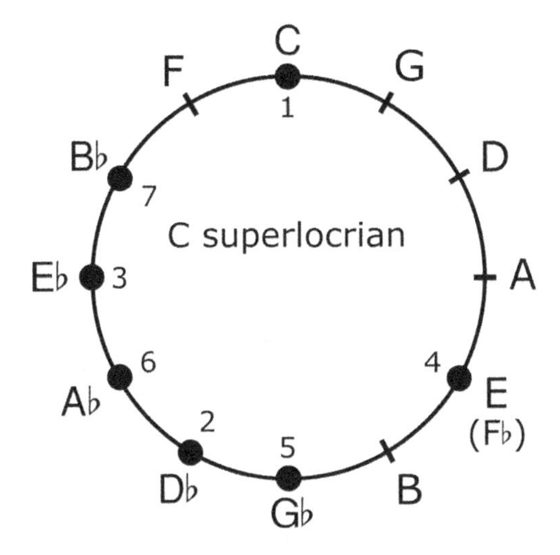


Figure 10.5: C diminished whole tone

Why bother with this one ? Because it speaks to many improvisation needs on altered dominant chords and also contains a pentatonic scale.

# The pentatonic scales

Pentatonic scales are widely used in folk music around the world and also for improvisation in jazz. The two most frequently used are the major and the minor pentatonics, the minor being the fifth mode of the major pentatonic.

The Circle of Fifths can also assist in visualising the choice of pentatonic scales available for improvising over a set of chord changes.

## The major pentatonic scale

The pentatonic major scale has the following melodic analysis, [3] based on the major scale with the same tonic : 1 2 3 5 6. Using C pentatonic major as an example, this scale consists of the sequence of five notes C D E G A.

You will recognise in these notes the same notes as a C major sixth chord with added ninth : C - E - G - A - D. This is another useful way to remember the pentatonic major scale.

You will also by now recognise that these notes correspond to a succession of four ascending intervals of a perfect fifth : C – G – D – A – E. As such, they can be readily placed on the circle of fifths in a pattern which is easily recalled. See Figure 10.6 below.

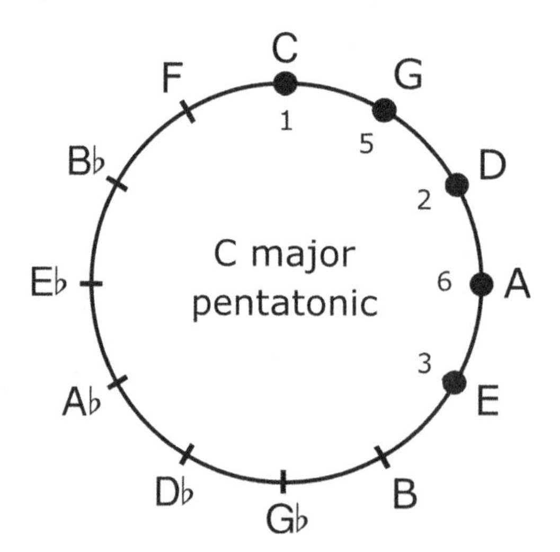


Figure 10.6: C pentatonic major scale

You may prefer to think in terms of five consecutive steps on the circle rather than four successive ascending intervals of a fifth.

3 See Introduction, page 2

For many purposes, it may well be sufficient to remember the note names in an unordered manner. In this case, just recall that a pentatonic major scale consists of the tonic + the next four note names in the clockwise direction round the circle. Thus, D pentatonic major scale will consist of the five notes D A E B F♯.

## The minor pentatonic scale

We said above that the pentatonic minor scale is the fifth mode of the pentatonic major scale. For C pentatonic major, C D E G A, the fifth mode will be A C D E G. This is the A pentatonic minor scale with melodic analysis 1 ♭3 4 5 ♭7 based on the corresponding A major scale (A B C♯ D E F♯ G♯ ). [4]

This is entirely analogous with the concept of major and relative minor as discussed above in Chapter 5.

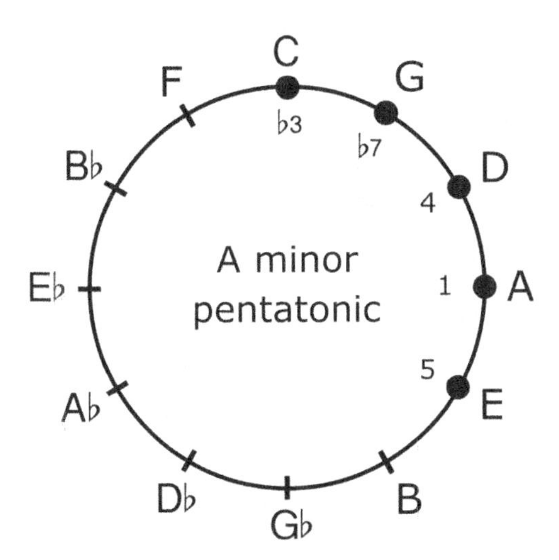


Figure 10.7: A pentatonic minor scale

In the same way that a major scale has a parallel minor, so the pentatonic major scale has a parallel pentatonic minor scale. In the case of C pentatonic major, we have C pentatonic minor and this is the following collection of notes : C E♭ F G B♭ with melodic analysis : 1 ♭3 4 5 ♭7.

This will be recognised as the fifth mode of E♭ pentatonic major scale which can also be thought of as the upper neighbour of C pentatonic major. [5]

The following Figure 10.8 shows two further examples : E♭ pentatonic major and C pentatonic minor. C pentatonic minor is the fifth mode of E♭ pentatonic major or, the other

4 See conventions, page 2
5 See Chapter 5 for the relatives

way round, E♭ pentatonic major is the second mode of C pentatonic minor. In each, we still have the same collection of note pitches, albeit unordered – four successive steps clockwise on the circle starting from the tonic of the major pentatonic scale.

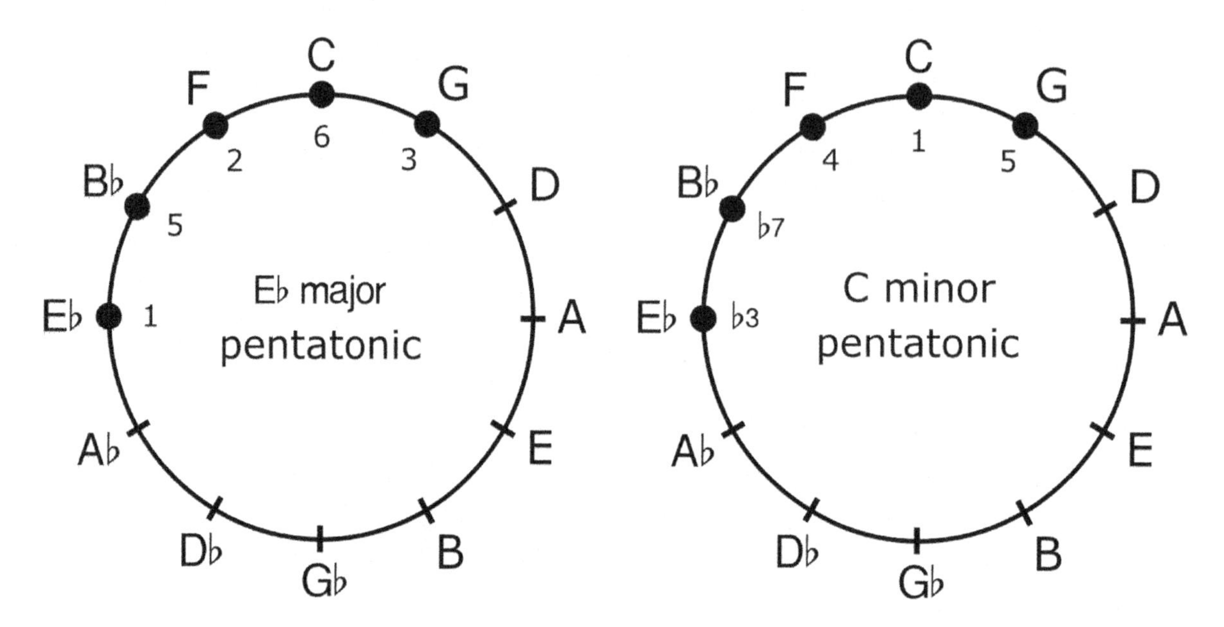


Figure 10.8: E♭ major pentatonic and C minor pentatonic

## The ♭3 pentatonic scale

Before leaving the pentatonics scales, I wish to note that jazz musicians will quite commonly use the ♭3 pentatonic scale. This is simply the major pentatonic which we have examined above but with the third degree flattened. Flattening the third degree gives this scale a minor or bluesy flavor.

This scale will not be formed of four consecutive ascending intervals of a perfect fifth (five adjacent notes on our circle). If you look at Figure 10.8 above, and imagine the E♭ major pentatonic becoming the E♭ flattened third pentatonic, you will arrive at the scale:

E♭ F G♭ B♭ C
1 2 ♭3 5 6

You will notice that it contains the tritone interval G♭ - C. Compare its structure with the Blues scale in the next section.

## The Blues scale

Although several variants of the Blues scale have developed over the years, the basic Blues scale perhaps most commonly used is based upon the minor pentatonic scale. It is a scale of six notes, the minor pentatonic plus the sharpened fourth (or flattened fifth). Its melodic analysis is 1 ♭3 4 ♭5 5 ♭7.

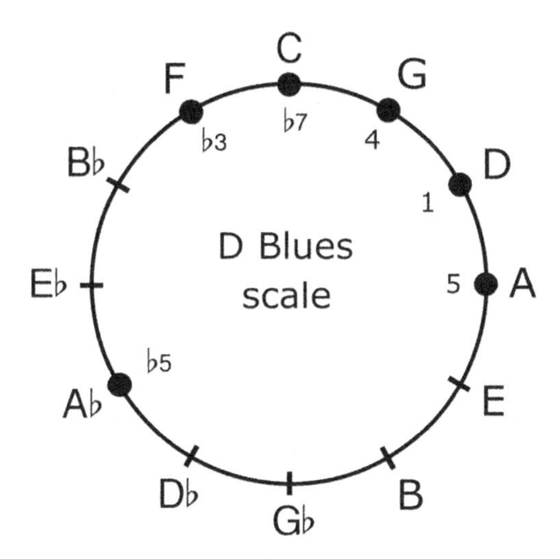


Figure 10.9: The D Blues scale

Figure 10.9 shows the case for the blues scale in D :

D F G A♭ A C
1 ♭3 4 ♭5 5 ♭7

You will see the D minor pentatonic scale + A♭, the flattened 5th. The flattened 5th together with the tonic form the interval of a tritone. This is quite clear in the drawing which shows the two notes at either end of a diameter on the circle.

# Choice of a pentatonic scale for improvisation.

First, let me be quite clear. I am not saying that there is a 'correct' or 'incorrect' scale for any given piece of harmony. The choice is up to the improviser who will have to decide if he wants to play 'in' or 'out'.

Some pentatonic scales will be more in than out when referenced to a particular passage of harmony. I will look first at the case of the diatonic major scales.

## Pentatonics and the major scales

From Figure 2.1 [6] where the degrees of the C Major scale are shown and from the description of the major pentatonic scale above on page 54, we can draw another circle diagram which will enable us to see easily and immediately which pentatonic major scales are contained within the diatonic major scale.

From this new circle, Figure 10.10, we can see that C Major scale 'occupies' exactly half of the circle and its area is delimited by the diameter representing its tritone, F – B. Because a major pentatonic scale is represented by 4 successive ascending perfect fifths, you will note that four such successive perfect fifths can be drawn from F, degree IV, from C, degree I and from G, degree V. This latter is marked in on the figure : G, D, A, E and B. These are the notes of the G pentatonic major scale : G A B D E.

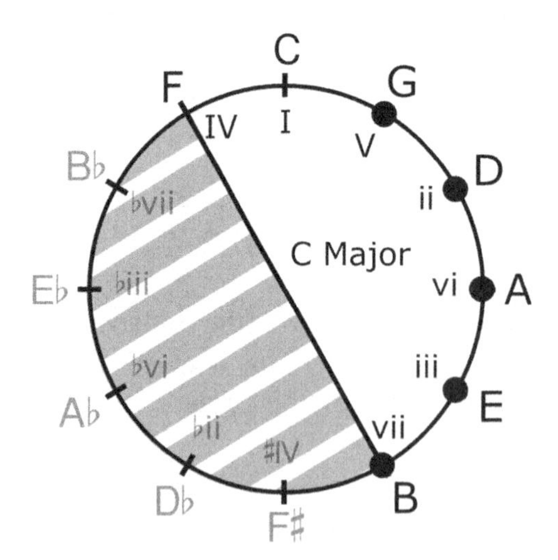


Figure 10.10: C Major with G pentatonic

Any other series of four fifths starting from D or from A or E or B will include the tritone interval from B to F and will not therefore be four successive perfect fifths.

6 Chapter 2, page 7

The three major pentatonic scales composed of notes diatonic to the C Major scale are :

- C pentatonic major : C D E G A
- F pentatonic major : F G A C D
- G pentatonic major : G A B D E

All three of these are 'in the key' and the choice of which to use will depend on other factors such as for example the chord progression. A ii – V – I progression might suggest a preference for the pentatonic on the V degree because of the absence of 'avoid' notes.

For any diatonic major scale, major pentatonic scales can be formed on the I, IV and V degrees.

Because the traditional modes use the same set of note pitches as the major scale, they can be represented on the circle by a rotation of the arrangement in Figure 10.10

Examples of pentatonic scales for the traditional modes are given below, in Appendix D.

## Pentatonics and the minor scales

Diatonic minor scales are usually more interesting because we have three possible variants which can be brought into play : the natural minor, the harmonic minor and the ascending melodic minor.

### *The natural minor*

The natural minor is another name for the traditional Aeolian mode and hence is formed by the same collection of pitches as the diatonic major scale and is its relative minor. The natural minor represents a displacement of all of the notes of the relative major scale by a minor third as shown here for C Major and its relative A minor -

| | | | 1 | 2 | 3 | 4 | 5 | 6 | 7 | 8 |
|---|---|---|---|---|---|---|---|---|---|---|
| | | C Major : | C | D | E | F | G | A | B | C |
| A minor : | A | B | C | D | E | F | G | A | | |
| | 1 | 2 | ♭3 | 4 | 5 | ♭6 | ♭7 | 8 | | |

Degree 1 of C Major becomes degree 3 of A minor ; generally referred to as ♭3 in accordance with convention which refers back each time to the major scale with the same tonic, A Major in this case.

The pentatonics on the 1st , 4th and 5th degrees : C pentatonic major, F pentatonic major, G pentatonic major in C Major are the same pentatonics in A minor but on the ♭3rd, ♭6th and ♭7th degrees : C pentatonic major, F pentatonic major, G pentatonic major.

You may prefer to think of them as minor pentatonics but as we have seen above, the minor pentatonic is the fifth mode of the major pentatonic so in A minor you may call them A pentatonic minor, D pentatonic minor and E pentatonic minor but the note pitch collections remain the same.

In this case, you will note that the minor pentatonics of A minor are on the same degrees as the major pentatonics of C Major : 1st, 4th and 5th degrees.

You can refer to Appendix D for a treatment of the pentatonics and the traditional modes.

### *The harmonic minor*

The harmonic minor is more interesting. Let us consider the case of C harmonic minor. This scale can be derived from C Major by flattening the 3rd and the 6th degrees, the 7th degree remains major : C D E♭ F G A♭ B. We plot this on the circle of fifths as Figure 10.11.

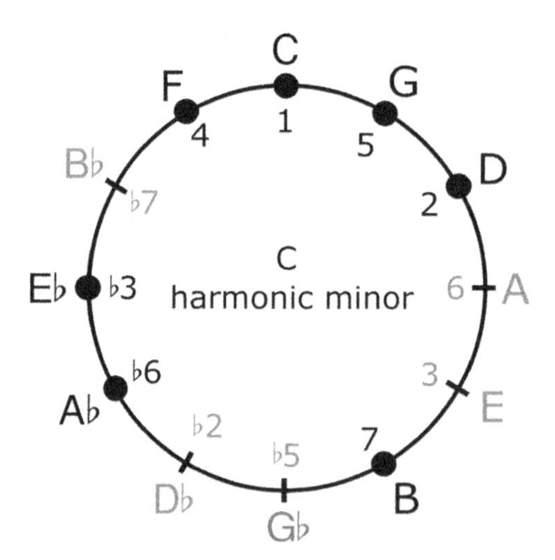


Figure 10.11: C harmonic minor

You will immediately spot that there is no group of four successive ascending intervals of perfect fifths and hence no standard pentatonic scale is contained within the harmonic minor scale.

## *The ascending melodic minor*

A similar treatment of C ascending melodic minor is shown below, Figure 10.12. C ascending melodic minor has only the 3rd degree flattened : C D E♭ F G A B.

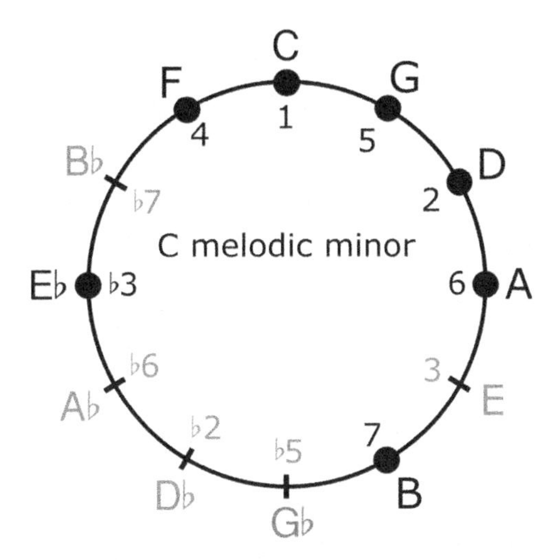


Figure 10.12: ascending melodic minor

In this scale, we have only one group of four successive ascending intervals of perfect fifths, F – C, C – G, G – D, D – A, and these are the notes of the pentatonic major scale of F, formed on the 4th degree : F G A C D.

Pentatonic major on F : F G A C D

For those of you who prefer to think in terms of minor pentatonic scales, this is the D minor pentatonic, D F G A C, formed on the 2nd degree of the melodic minor scale.

All ascending melodic minor scales contain only one pentatonic scale.

## Pentatonics and the diminished whole tone scale

The diminished whole tone scale also known as the Superlocrian or altered scale has important uses in improvisation in passages using altered dominant chords. The C diminished whole tone scale is shown below.

C D♭ E♭ F♭ G♭ A♭ B♭ C
1 ♭2 ♭3 ♭4 ♭5 ♭6 ♭7 8

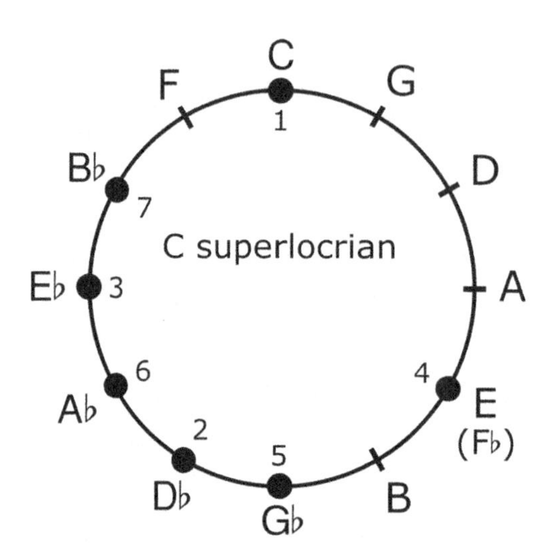


Figure 10.13: C diminished whole tone scale

From the series of four ascending perfect fifth intervals on the left hand side of the circle, you will see that this scale contains only one pentatonic major scale starting on the 5th degree, G♭ pentatonic major :

G♭ A♭ B♭ D♭ E♭

The Superlocrian can be considered a minor mode and you may prefer to think minor pentatonic scale. In this case, we have E♭ minor pentatonic on the 3rd degree of the scale :

E♭ G♭ A♭ B♭ D♭

The diminished whole tone scale contains only one major pentatonic scale.

Exercise material on the contents of this chapter is available in *The Workbook: Volume 2 – Further Steps.*

# 11 - Chord scales

For improvising musicians, whether wishing to play 'in' or 'out', it is essential to understand what set of notes are available to use at any moment. This is decided both by the harmonic structure of the piece and by the content of the melody and not just by the the key as indicated by the key signature.

Quite apart from considerations of the overall form of the piece, for example AABA where the B section may well be in a different key from the A sections, local chord progressions within a section may indicate a temporary change of key for a series of measures without a modulation having been formally declared.

Other factors which can intervene are the borrowing of chords from related scales or modes and too, the player has to decide whether the context is tonal or modal.

### Where did that chord come from?

A frequently occurring question is : Where did that chord come from ? And here, as you might expect by now, the circle of fifths offers some visual help. We'll look first at the case of major scales. The harmonisation of minor scales is more complicated because of the existence of three versions, Natural minor, Harmonic minor, Melodic minor, not to mention other minor modes.

## Major triads and seventh chords in major scales

### Major triads

If you remember the harmonisation of the major scales, touched on briefly in the Introduction [1], you will know that a diatonic major triad may be constructed on the first, fourth and fifth degrees in a major key.

Thus, a major triad with root C can have a harmonic function of I , IV or V in a major key. Three tonal scale possibilities therefore exist for this major triad with root C :

I of C Major ; IV of G Major ; V of F Major

The following illustration, Figure 11.1, shows three examples as you can envisage them on the circle of fifths. The first thing you will notice is that the degrees I, IV, V are arranged in a mirror image compared with what we introduced in Chapter 2, Figure 2.1. This is because we are asking a different question. In Chapter 2, we were asking “What degree in the C Ma-

1 See Introduction, Page 2

jor scale does this note represent ?" Here, we are asking "In what major scale does C fall on degree I (or IV or V) ?"

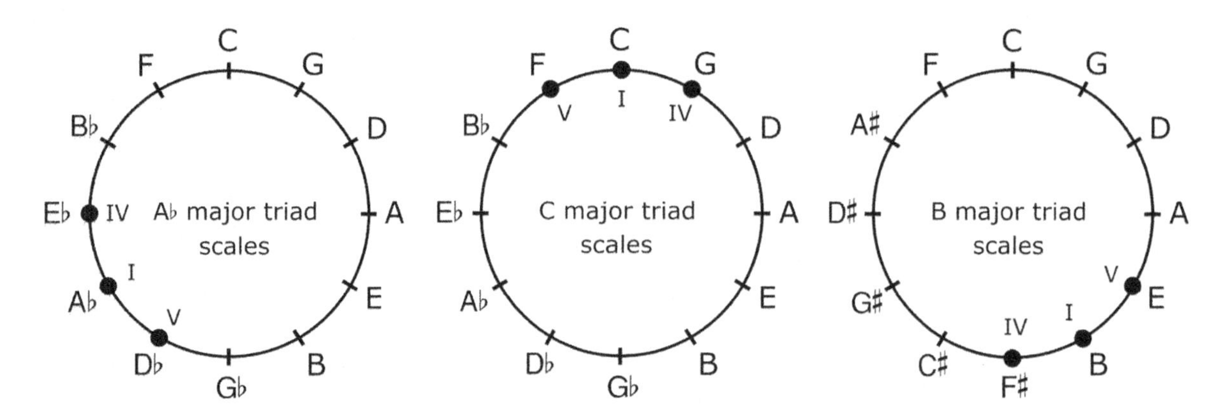


Figure 11.1: Examples of major chord scales for major triads

Figure 11.1 shows that for a major triad with root A♭, it can have a tonic function I in A♭ Major, a dominant function V in D♭ Major, a sub-dominant function IV in E♭ Major.

Similarly a C major triad can be : I in C Major, IV in G Major or V in F Major.

The third example is for a B major triad : I in B Major, IV in F♯ Major or V in E Major.

Thus for any given root note name on the circle, the triad can be the tonic of a major scale with the same name, the sub-dominant of a major scale one step round to the right, or the dominant of a major scale one step around the circle to the left.

## Major seventh chords

In a major scale, only two degrees can support a diatonic major seventh chord, I and IV. Figure 11.2 shows examples for three different major seventh chords.

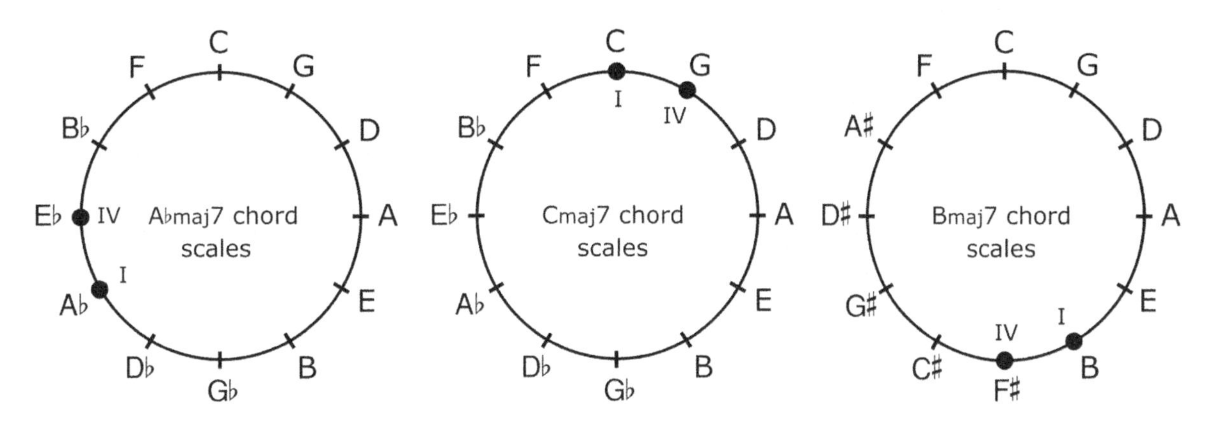


Figure 11.2: Examples of major chord scales for major seventh chords

Figure 11.2 shows that for a major seventh chord with root A♭, it can have a tonic function I in A♭ Major or a sub-dominant function IV in E♭ Major.

Similarly a C major seventh chord can be : I in C Major or IV in G Major.

The third example is for a B major seventh chord : I in B Major or IV in F♯ Major.

Thus for any given root note name on the circle, the major seventh chord can be the tonic of a major scale with the same name or the sub-dominant of a major scale one step round to the right.

## Dominant seventh chords

In a major scale, only one degree supports a diatonic dominant seventh chord, the fifth degree,V. For any given root note name on the circle, the dominant seventh chord is the dominant of a major scale one step round the circle to the left. Figure 11.3 shows this case for a C7 chord.

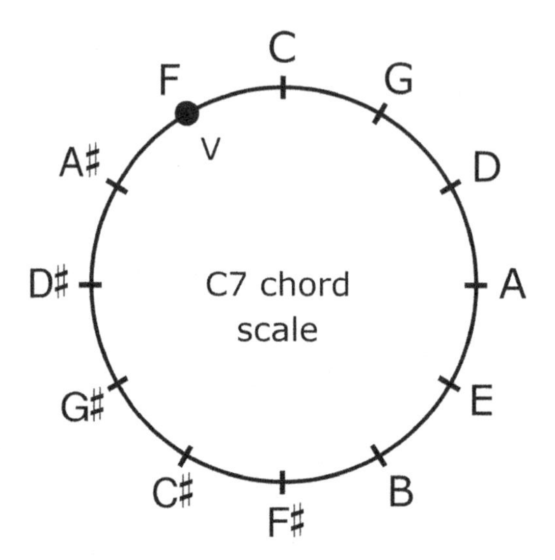


Figure 11.3: a dominant seventh chord scale

C7 is the fifth degree of F Major scale. This, of course, is just another way of looking at the most basic use of the circle of fifths.

## Minor triads and seventh chords in major scales

In major scales, if the triad is minor then the seventh chord will also be minor and this applies to chords constructed on the second, third and sixth degrees : harmonic functions of ii, iii or vi.

For a minor chord with a given tonic, the scale concerned is either 2 steps to the left for the ii function, 3 steps to the left for the vi function or 4 steps to the left for the iii function.

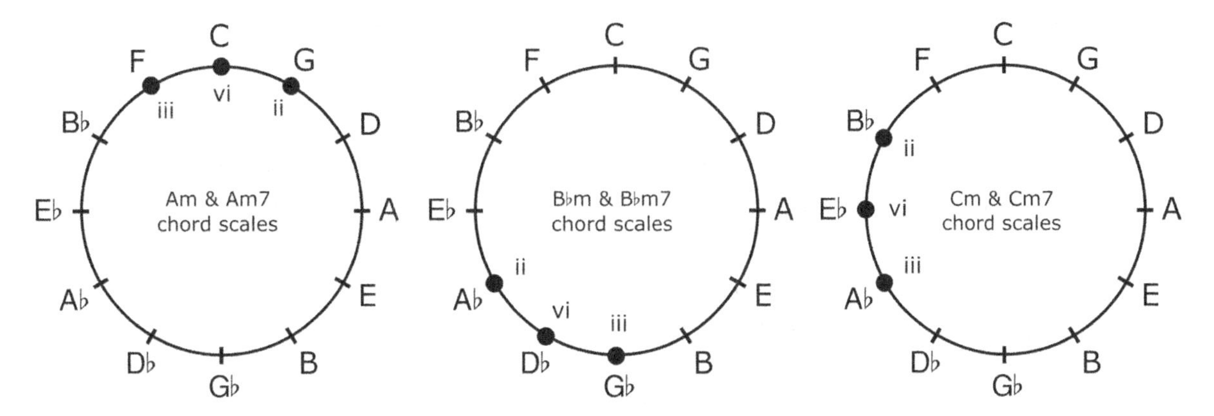


Figure 11.4: examples of minor chord scales

Figure 11.4 shows examples for minor chords with three different roots :

Am and Am7 chords can have a ii harmonic function in G Major scale (2 steps left), a iii function in F Major scale (4 steps to the left) or a vi function in C Major scale (3 steps to the left).

B♭m and B♭m7 chords can have a ii harmonic function in A♭ Major scale, a iii function in G♭ Major scale or a vi function in D♭ Major scale.

Cm and Cm7 chords can have a ii harmonic function in B♭ Major scale, a iii function in A♭ Major scale or a vi function in E♭ Major scale.

## An example of pentatonic scale selection for minor seventh chords

Always bearing in mind the caveat that there is no absolute choice but rather the ear and the intention of the performer should be the deciding factors. Using information covered in this chapter and in chapter 10, let us try to determine some appropriate pentatonic scales for use in improvising over a B♭m7 chord. To simplify, we will consider major scales.

First, from figure 11.4 above, you will see that B♭m7 can arrive in three cases where it is diatonic to a major scale :

- as the ii of A♭ Major
- as the vi of D♭ Major
- as the iii of G♭ Major

Now, let us recall which major pentatonics are inside or diatonic to each of these three major scales. You are referred back to Chapter 10. The major pentatonics are formed on the I, IV and V degrees of each major scale.

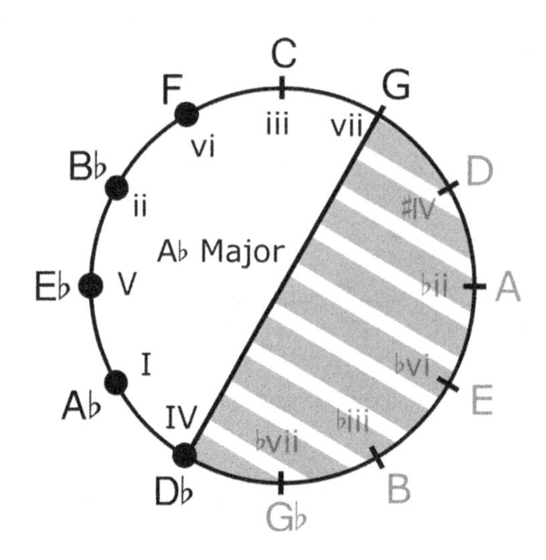


Figure 11.5: A♭ Major scale and Db major pentatonic

You will recall that IV and V are either side of the tonic on the circle : IV is one step to the left of I and V is 1 step to the right. [2]

In figure 11.5 above, D♭ pentatonic major is shown by the large dots starting on the degree IV of A♭ Major.

So taking into account the three major scales, G♭ Major, D♭ Major, A♭ Major each having three diatonic pentatonic major scales, this gives us the choice of 5 different pentatonic majors :

| | |
|---|---|
| from G♭ Major : | G♭ , C♭ , D♭ pentatonic majors |
| from D♭ Major : | D♭ , G♭ , A♭ pentatonic majors |
| from A♭ Major : | A♭ , D♭ , E♭ pentatonic majors |

D♭ pentatonic major occurs 3 times, G♭ and A♭ 2 times each and E♭ and C♭ only once each. As a first approximation, it could be reasonable to consider that for a chord of B♭m7, D♭ pentatonic major (or its relative minor B♭ pentatonic minor) could be a good inside choice.

D♭ E♭ F A♭ B♭

This analysis can be summed up as using the pentatonic major on the ♭3 of the m7 chord.

2 See Figure 2.1

It must be repeated that the above is valid in the absence of other information which might influence the performer's choice in a different direction.

# Harmonisation of the minor scales

In addition to the major and minor perfect triads and the diminished triad found in the harmonisation of the major scale, the richer harmonisation of the three main versions of the minor scale also includes the augmented triad. The situation with seventh chords is even richer due to the various modified degrees : ♭3 in all three minor scales, ♭6 and ♭7 in the natural minor, ♭6 in the harmonic minor.

In addition to the three seventh chords with a perfect fifth and the seventh chord with a diminished fifth (m7♭5), the minor harmonisations add the following :

- perfect minor triad with major seventh (m.maj7),

and two more with altered fifths :

- the diminished seventh (dim7)
- the major seventh with sharpened fifth (maj7♯5).

## The natural minor

The natural minor is the Aeolian (sixth) mode of the major scale [3]. As such, it adds nothing more to the harmonisation of the major scale but is a simple linear displacement of the degrees.

| | | | | | | | | | | |
|---|---|---|---|---|---|---|---|---|---|---|
| | | | 1 | 2 | 3 | 4 | 5 | 6 | 7 | 8 |
| | | E♭ Major : | E♭ | F | G | A♭ | B♭ | C | D | E♭ |
| C minor : | C | D | E♭ | F | G | A♭ | B♭ | C | | |
| | 1 | 2 | ♭3 | 4 | 5 | ♭6 | ♭7 | 8 | | |

So the harmonisation of C minor produces the same chords as E♭ Major but on different degrees :

| | | | | | | | | |
|---|---|---|---|---|---|---|---|---|
| E♭ Major | I | ii | iii | IV | V | vi | vii | |
| C minor nat. | vi | vii | I | ii | iii | IV | V | equivalent E♭ Major degrees |

For example : the triad on the tonic of C natural minor is C - E♭ - G, ie Cm and this is the same chord formed on the sixth degree of E♭ Major.

3 For notes on the modes, see Appendix C

## The harmonic minor

This scale is a variation of the natural minor scale with a major seventh : 1 2 ♭3 4 5 ♭6 7

This produces the following changes in diatonic chord construction :

- the 1st degree gives a minor triad but a m.maj7 seventh chord
- the 3rd degree gives an augmented triad and a maj7♯5 seventh chord
- the 5th degree has a perfect major triad and a dominant seventh chord
- the 7th degree has a diminished triad and a diminished seventh chord

Perhaps the most significant chord of the harmonic minor is the V7♭9 chord on the 5th degree. When you see a V7♭9 chord, it is a good indicator of a harmonic minor scale.

## The melodic minor (ascending)

This scale is another variant this time differing from the harmonic minor in having a major sixth as well as a major seventh : 1 2 ♭3 4 5 6 7. This implies the following changes to the harmonisation with respect to the natural minor :

- the 1st degree has a perfect minor triad and a m.maj7 seventh chord
- the 2nd degree has a perfect minor triad and a minor seventh chord
- the 3rd degree has an augmented triad and a maj7♯5 seventh chord
- the 4th degree has a perfect major triad and a dominant seventh
- the 5th degree has a perfect major triad and a dominant seventh
- the 6th degree has a diminished triad and a half-diminished seventh
- the 7th degree has a diminished triad and a half-diminished seventh

## The melodic minor descending

This scale is the same as the natural minor scale.

# Altered dominant chords

Chords like C7♯5 or A9♯5 are typically associated with the whole tone scale. They may feature in jazz pieces as intermediate chords in a bass line descending by semitones, for instance, where their neutral even floating character will not impinge on the current tonality.

Consider the altered ninth chord D9♯5 : this consists of the following pitch elements if the 7th is also included -

D - F♯ - A♯ - C - E

These notes are only missing the G♯ of the whole tone scale : D E F♯ G♯ A♯ C which itself is a mode of the C whole tone scale. [4]

## The altered dominant

A chord of the form C7♭9 ♯9 ♯11 ♭13 has all the alterations possible. This will be used with the diminished whole tone scale. Here is the C diminished whole tone scale we saw in Chapter 10 [5], C D♭ E♭ F♭ G♭ A♭ B♭, but with some notes respelled together with its melodic analysis below :

C D♭ D♯ E F♯ A♭ B♭
1 ♭9 ♯9 3 ♯11 ♭13 ♭7

You will see that this corresponds exactly with the (extremely) altered dominant chord.

## Further resource

A short notice showing the harmonizations of the major and minor scales is available for download. See Appendix E.

Exercise material on the harmonisation of the major scale is covered in *The Workbook: Volume 2 – Further Steps.*

Exercise material on the minor scale is covered in *The Workbook: Volume 3 – Minor & More.*

4 See Chapter 10, page 49
5 See page 53

Notes

# 12 - Quartal Harmony

Harmony based on chords built from fourths certainly appeared long ago in musical compositions. Schoenberg et al used them early in the 20$^{th}$ century but they became really popular with the move towards modal music, lead among others by Miles Davis in the 1960's.

For a recap on the modes, see the Appendix C.

The intervals employed in a chord made of fourths may be 'perfect fourths', 'augmented fourths' or combinations of perfect and augmented fourths. The augmented fourth is one expression of the tritone which has already been discussed in Chapter 7 above. A 'diminished fourth' has the same intervallic size as a major third and is generally considered as belonging to tertian harmony. These latter may of course be combined with perfect or augmented fourths but are not the subject of this section.

We have seen in Chapter 10 above, in the section on 'pentatonics and the major scales', how easily the circle of fifths can be used to visualise which major pentatonic scales are present within each Major scale. Figure 10.10 was used to illustrate this for the C Major scale.

We can use a similar diagram to illustrate how quartal chords may be assembled within a major scale, which diatonic combinations will be all perfect fourths and which will include the tritone. Below, Figure 12.1 is based upon Figure 10.10.

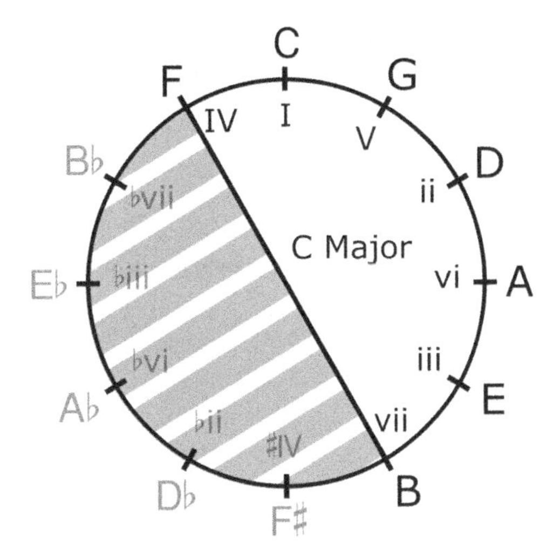


Figure 12.1: C Major scale elements

The seven note pitches of any diatonic major scale occupy half of the circle of fifths bounded by the diameter drawn between the IV$^{th}$ and vii$^{th}$ degrees (the tritone interval present in all diatonic major scales). The IV$^{th}$ degree is one step anti-clockwise from the tonic degree and the vii$^{th}$ is five steps clockwise round the circle from the tonic. If we start from the vii$^{th}$ degree, B in the case of C Major, each step anti-clockwise represents a perfect fourth upwards. [1]

So, the following three-note quartal chords are composed of successive perfect fourth intervals :

- B – E – A
- E – A – D
- A – D – G
- D – G – C
- G – C – F

and these three-note quartal chords contain the tritone interval :

- C – F – B
- F – B – E

In a similar fashion, we can visualise 4 four-note quartal chords composed of successive perfect fourths and 3 four-note quartal chords which contain a tritone.

You will note that there are also 3 five-note quartal chords composed of successive perfect fourths :

1. B – E – A – D – G
2. E – A – D – G – C
3. A – D – G – C – F

1 Direction of fourths ascending : Chapter 4, page 15

Now, you can associate them with the three major pentatonic scales which can be formed from each diatonic major scale.

1. B – E – A – D – G → G pentatonic major on V : G A B D E
2. E – A – D – G – C → C pentatonic major on I : C D E G A
3. A – D – G – C – F → F pentatonic major on IV : F G A C D

Refresh your memory, perhaps, by reference to Chapter 10, above. [2]

Similarly, the six note quartal chord B - E - A - D - G - C can transform easily into the C whole note scale by simple lowering by a semitone three of its members. The whole note scale is a combination of two augmented triads. [3] See figure 12.2 below.

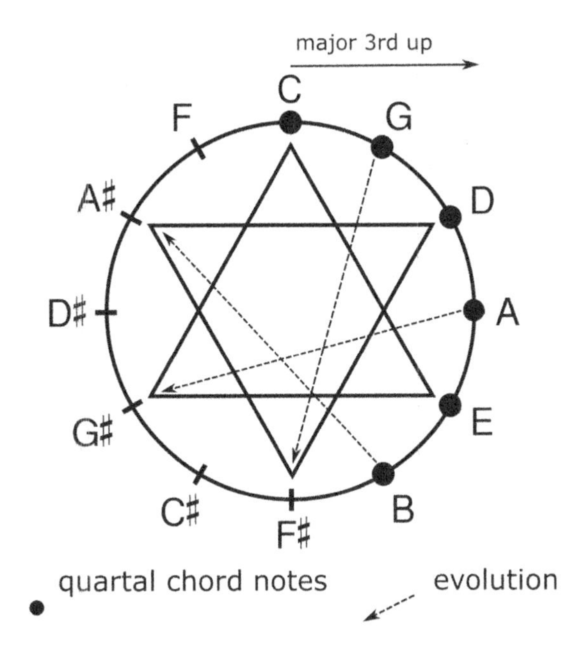


Figure 12.2: quartal chords and whole tone scale

Lowering by a semitone of G to F♯, A to G♯ and B to A♯ transforms the six note quartal chord to the C whole tone scale : C D E F♯ G♯ A♯.

2 Pentatonics and the major scales : page 54
3 Whole tone scale and augmented triads : page 49

The same is true for the other 6 note quartal chord : E - A - D - G - C - F. Lowering C, D and E by a semitone transforms it to the D♭ whole tone scale :

D♭ E♭ F G A B

Similar transformations can be made by raising three of the quartal chord notes a semitone.

Exercise material on the contents of this chapter is covered in *The Workbook: Volume 3 – Minor & More.*

# 13 - Transposing Instruments

Transposing instruments are those which emit a sound different from that which the player reads and plays on his part. The transpositions most commonly used in musical instruments are B♭ and E♭. This means that when the player of a B♭ instrument such as a clarinet or trumpet reads a note C and plays C, the sound emitted will be a B♭, a major second lower. For an E♭ instrument such as the alto-sax, the player will read and play C but the sound produced will be E♭, a major sixth lower.

Other instrument transpositions exist, for example : clarinet in A, clarinet in G, trumpet in D, French horns in F. But the B♭ and E♭ are by far the most common so I shall restrict our examples to those two.

Non-transposing instruments are referred to as 'concert pitch' instruments and include flutes, trombones, guitars, piano, clarinet in C. Some instruments, such as the guitar, sound an octave lower than written on the score. Others, like the baritone sax in E♭ sound a major sixth plus an octave lower and the tenor sax in B♭ sounds a major second plus an octave lower. The octave part does not generally present any conceptual difficulty with which the circle of fifths can help. Although the complete transposition must be taken into account for orchestration and arranging purposes, we shall not be considering in this chapter, the octave part of the transpositions.

Any instrument playing on its own or with a similar group of instruments can play in any key available to that instrument. The need to transpose arrives when different classes of transposing or concert pitch instruments are required to play together. In the case of a trombone playing a piece of music in company with a B♭ trumpet and an alto-sax, if each player shares the partition written for the trombone player, when they each read and blow a note C, the trombone will sound a C, the trumpet will sound a B♭ and the alto-sax an E♭. The result may or may not be pleasing but it will not be the result expected by the composer.

To make a C sound come out of each instrument, the trombone player will blow a C, the trumpet player must blow a note a major second higher, D, and the alto-sax player must play a note a major sixth higher, an A. The trumpet transposes the note a major second down and the alto-sax a major sixth down.

For the playing musician, his partition is usually provided ready printed in the transposition required for his instrument. If, however, only a concert pitch part is available, the B♭ and E♭ players will need to transpose their parts to an appropriate key. Fortunately, the choice of key follows the logic already outlined above for individual notes. As the trumpet player had to play a note a major second higher, D, in order to sound a C, so if the trombone player's part is written in C Major, the trumpet player's part will have to be written in D Major.

For the purpose of choosing the appropriate key, the circle of fifths is not really indispensable but can be brought into use for rapid visualisation as I shall demonstrate in the following paragraphs. Some additional material to help avoid the complications of double sharps and flats is available for free download. See the Resources section in Appendix E.

We shall be moving the playing key up or down by various intervals. To review the sense in which different intervals move up or down on the circle of fifths, refer back to Chapter 4.

## From concert pitch to B♭ transposition

The part in concert pitch must be transposed to a key having its tonic a major second higher for the B♭ instrument. In Figure 13.1 we have restated the number of sharps and flats for each of the keys [1] and you can see that to move up a major second means a move of 2 steps clockwise around the circle. That means 2 flats fewer or two sharps more than the concert pitch key (or one flat less plus one sharp more). Thus, to obtain the key needed by a B♭ instrument, move two steps clockwise around the circle from the concert pitch key to find the transposed key a major second higher.

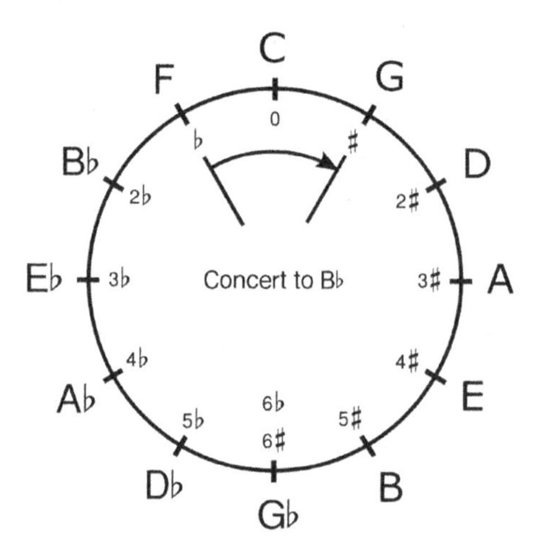


Figure 13.1: Concert pitch to B♭ instrument

Figure 13.1 shows the case of a piece of music in concert pitch of F Major which must be transposed up a major second to the key of G Major for a B♭ transposing instrument, such as a clarinet in B♭.

1 See Chapter 3

## From concert pitch to E♭ transposition

When a player of an E♭ instrument fingers F and blows F, his instrument sounds A♭, a major sixth lower. So, in order to sound an F, the player has to blow a note a major sixth higher, D.

The part in concert pitch must be transposed to a key having its tonic a major sixth higher for the E♭ instrument. In Figure 13.2 you can see that to move up a major sixth means a move of 3 steps clockwise around the circle. That means 3 flats fewer or 3 sharps more than the concert pitch key (or combinations of fewer flats and more sharps totalling three).

Thus, to obtain the key needed by an E♭ instrument, move three steps clockwise around the circle from the concert pitch key to find the transposed key a major sixth higher.

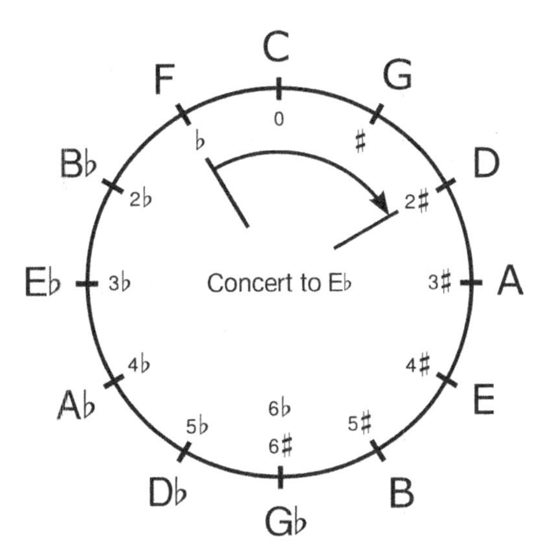


Figure 13.2: Concert pitch to E♭ instrument

Figure 13.2 shows the case of piece in concert pitch F Major which must be transposed up a major sixth to the key of D Major for an E♭ transposing instrument, such as as an E♭ alto-saxophone.

## From B♭ to E♭ transpositions

The part produced for a B♭ transposing instrument must be transposed to a key having 1 flat fewer or one sharp more in order to be played by an E♭ transposing instrument. To do this on the circle of fifths, move one step clockwise from the B♭ instrument's key. That is, move up to a key a perfect fifth higher.

By comparing Figure 13.1 with Figure 13.2, you will see that an instrument in concert pitch will be playing in F Major while the B♭ trumpet will be playing in G Major and the alto-sax will be playing in D Major.

## From B♭ transposition to concert pitch

For the reverse operation, the part for the B♭ transposing instrument must be transposed to a key having its tonic a major second lower. In Figure 13.3 you can see that to move down a major second means a move of 2 steps anti-clockwise around the circle. That means 2 flats more or two sharps fewer than the key for the B♭ instrument (or one more flat and one less sharp). Thus, to obtain the key needed by a concert pitch instrument, move two steps anti-clockwise around the circle from the B♭ instrument's key to find the concert pitch key a major second lower.

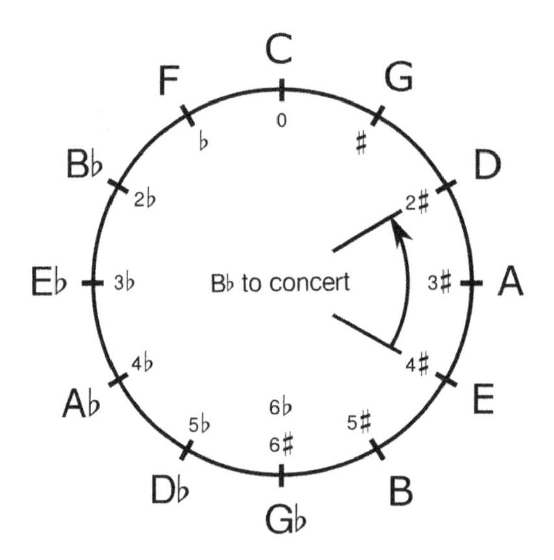


Figure 13.3: B♭ instrument to concert pitch

Figure 13.3 shows an example where a part for a B♭ transposing instrument in the key of E Major has to be transposed down by a major second to the key of D Major for a concert pitch instrument.

## From E♭ transposition to concert pitch

The part for an E♭ transposing instrument must be transposed to a key having its tonic a major sixth lower for the concert pitch instrument. In Figure 13.4 you can see that to move down a major sixth means a move of 3 steps anti-clockwise around the circle. That means 3 flats more or 3 sharps fewer than the key for the E♭ instrument (or combinations of more flats and fewer sharps totalling three). Thus, to obtain the key needed by a concert pitch instrument, move three steps anti-clockwise around the circle from the E♭ instrument's key to find the concert pitch key a major sixth lower.

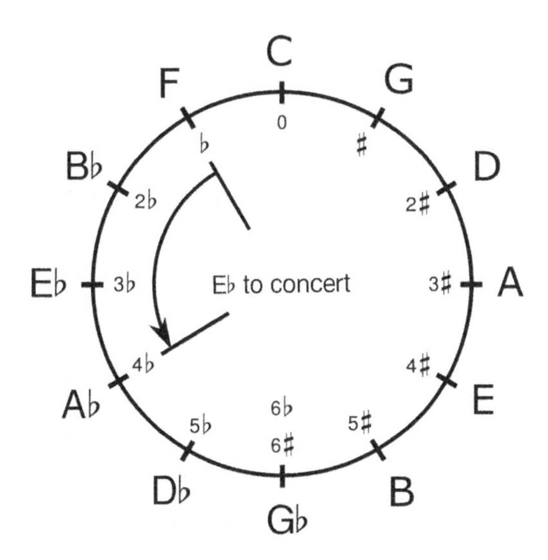


Figure 13.4: E♭ instrument to concert pitch

Figure 13.4 shows an example where a part for an E♭ transposing instrument in the key of F Major has to be transposed down by a major sixth to the key of A♭ Major for a concert pitch instrument.

## From E♭ to B♭ transpositions

The part produced for an E♭ transposing instrument must be transposed to a key having 1 flat more or one sharp fewer in order to be played by a B♭ transposing instrument. To do this on the circle of fifths, move one step anti-clockwise from the E♭ instrument's key. That is, move down to a key a perfect fifth lower.

Exercise material on the contents of this chapter is covered in *The Workbook: Volume 3 – Minor & More.*

# Your next steps

And you can continue your musical journey with exercises from The Workbooks in the Visual Tools for Musicians Series. *The Workbooks* are accessible and straightforward accompanying guides designed to solidify key concepts. Paralleling the tone of the parent volume, Jackson encourages diving in and developing skills with exercises and additional tutelage. And by following his practical solutions to common pitfalls, you'll soon gain clarity and approach your new passion fearlessly.

*The Workbook: Volume 1 - Early Steps* is the ideal interactive tool for hitting all the right notes. If you like concrete examples, learning through applying principles, and exciting alternative teaching methods, then you'll love Philip Jackson's finely tuned handbook.

**Check out the series here: https://www.amazon.com/gp/product/B095X3MVRZ**

**or use the QR code**

# Other Books

To complement and reinforce the learning process in this book, I have extended the Visual Tools for Musicians Series by the addition of three workbooks of exercises. These follow this book, *The Circle of Fifths*, chapter by chapter and each workbook is in two parts: exercises and worked answers. Additional explanations have been added to the answers where it has been found to be useful.

## The Workbooks : visual tools series

- **The Workbook: Volume 1 – Early Steps** – contains over 60 new exercises with model answers covering chapters 1 through 7 of *The Circle of Fifths.*

Available in paperback and ebook formats : https://www.amazon.com/dp/B093Z9TLFF

- **The Workbook: Volume 2 – Further Steps** – 64 new exercises with model answers covering chapters 8 to 11 (Major scale part) of *The Circle of Fifths.*

Available in paperback and ebook formats: https://www.amazon.com/dp/B094DM77C5

- **The Workbook: Volume 3 – Minor & More** – 78 new exercises with model answers covering chapters 11 (minor scales) through 13 of *The Circle of Fifths.*

Available in paperback and ebook formats: https://www.amazon.com/dp/B094P2H5ML

## Notes on Music Theory Series

- **Why Scales Need Sharps and Flats** – a detailed look at the construction of our fundamental reference, the major scale.

Available in paperback and ebook formats: https://www.amazon.com/dp/B08JKSFC4K

### also in French :

**Le Cycle des Quintes** – https://www.amazon.fr/dp/B019889RE4

**Pourquoi dièses et bémols dans des gammes** – https://www.amazon.fr/dp/B08NZV96JS

Notes

# - Appendices

## Appendix A - the harmonic series

In the natural world, sounds are impure unlike some sounds which can be produced by a synthesiser. The sounding of a fundamental tone gives rise, at the same time, to the creation of a whole series of other sounds originally named overtones. This name has tended to give way somewhat to the more generalised description 'members of the harmonic series'. We shall see why later.

The importance of the 'fifth' is that it is the first non-octave member of the harmonic series of sounds generated when a fundamental note is sounded. It is therefore the most easily heard overtone. When the note C is sounded (on a piano, clarinet, stretched string or whatever), the first overtone is C an octave higher followed by G and the higher members of the harmonic series.

When the note G is sounded, the first overtone is another G, an octave higher followed by D and the higher members of the series.

Taking the early members of the harmonic series generated by the root or fundamental, C, we have in order :

C, C, G, C, E, G, B♭, C, D, E, F♯, G, A, B♭, B, C ......

You can see where they could be situated on the staves of our written system in the illustration below, Figure 15.1.

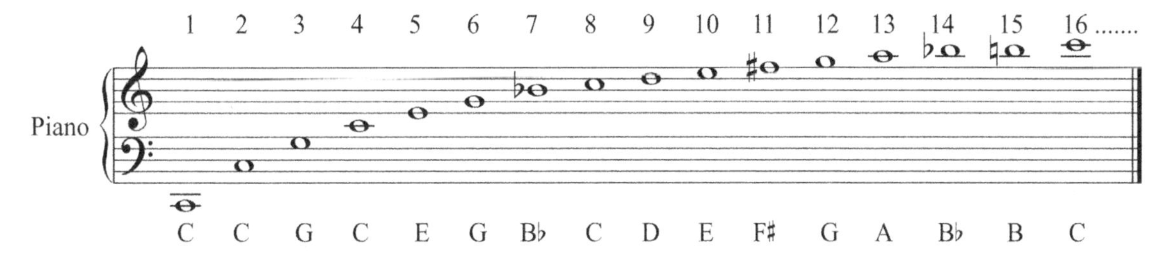


Figure 1: Members of the harmonic series on a fundamental note of C

Note that it takes four octaves to cover the first 16 members of the series.

Here, we can show the interest in numbering all the members of the harmonic series starting from the root or fundamental. The same named note an octave higher has a frequency two times the frequency of the lower note. The second member of the series is a C, an octave higher than the fundamental. The fourth member is a C with frequency twice that of the second member. The third member is a G with frequency 1.5 times that of the second member, C. Thus the ranking numbers of the members of the harmonic series can be used to determine the frequency. The frequency, f, of member n is n/(n-1) x the frequency of member n-1.

$$f_n = n/(n-1)\, f_{n-1}$$

# Appendix B - the order of semitones

We will look briefly at the circle and semitones, both descending and ascending. Whereas it is not particularly practical to use the circle for quick visualisation of the semitone interval, by exploring how they are arranged on the circle, we shall uncover an interesting relationship between the chromatic scale and the tritone.

If you start, for example, from C and proceed to the right (clockwise) for 5 steps round the circle, you arrive at B which is one semitone down from C, Figure 15.2. A semitone is a minor second and we have seen in Chapter 4, page 15, that minor intervals descend in a clockwise direction on our circle.

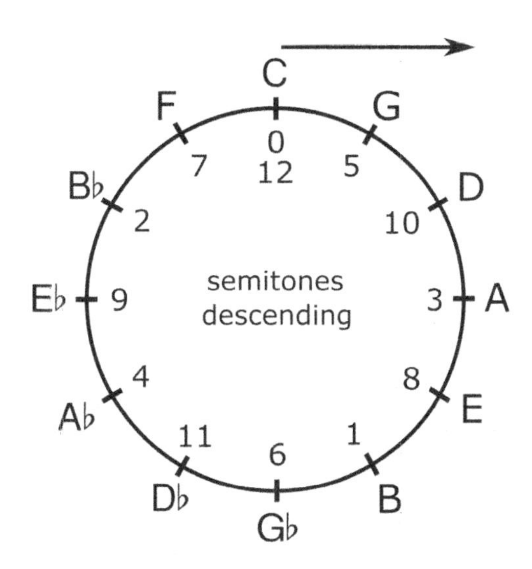


Figure 2: Descending semitones from C

Proceed a further five steps and you arrive at B♭, 2 semitones down from C. Each group of 5 steps clockwise takes you down another semitone.

What we are doing, in fact, is each time we move five steps clockwise round our circle of fifths, we are ascending through five intervals of a perfect fifth : C to G, G to D, D to A, A to E, E to B. Moving clockwise up through five fifths takes us through to the end of a third octave. See this illustrated in Figure 15.3.

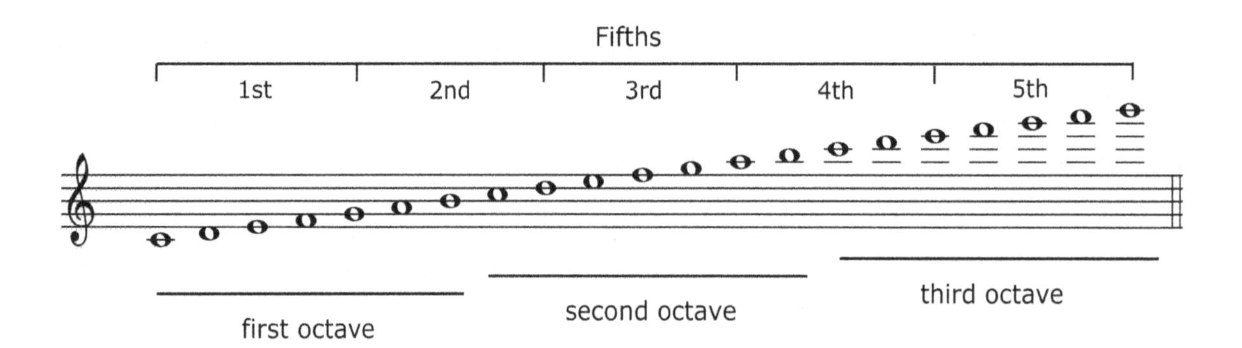


Figure 3: 1 semitone is five fifths up and that is three octaves

To understand this, look at the series of intervals involved. C – G is an interval of a fifth. C – D is an interval of a ninth (octave + major second). C – A is an interval of a 13th (octave + major sixth). C – E is an interval of a 17th (2 octaves + major third). C – B is an interval of a 21st (2 octaves + major seventh).

Thus every displacement of five steps round to the right involves a descent from the starting point of one semitone.

Moving in the anticlockwise direction through five steps takes us up one semitone from the starting point, C in the case of Figure 15.4. This is entirely symmetrical with the descending case above.

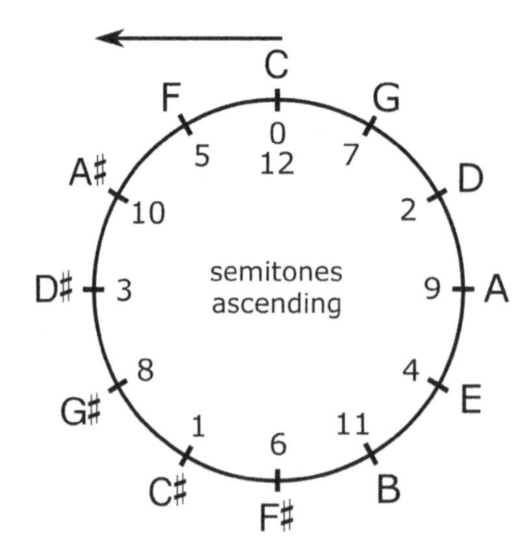


Figure 4: Ascending semitones from C

What you can see in addition to the simple observation of descending or ascending semitones in Figures 15.2 and 15.4 and their placement on the circle of fifths is the relationship between these figures and the chromatic scale.

This relationship is down to tritone inversion. [1] If in either of Figures 15.2 or 15.4 we do an inversion of the tritone on alternate notes on the circle, beginning with G, we end up with a representation of the chromatic scale.

Exchange : G and D♭, A and E♭, B and F and we arrive at Figure 15.5 below.

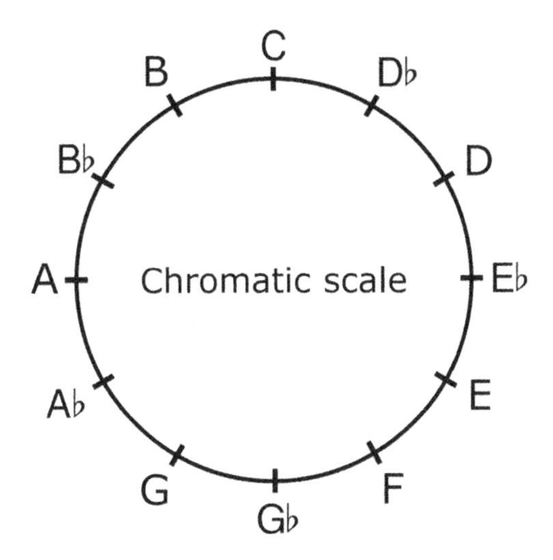


Figure 5: the chromatic scale

1 See Chapter 6 for the tritone

# Appendix C – some remarks on the modes

We will look first at the make up of each mode then at an alternative way of arriving rapidly at a desired mode. Finally we will show on the circle how the modes relate to each other and to the order of increasing number of flats.

A scale, in terms of a succession of notes, is said to be a mode of another scale if it consists of the same notes in the same order but starting on a different member of the series.

## Modes of the major scale

In modern usage, the modes of the major scale are named after the ancient Greek modes and these names were also used by the Christian churches in medieval times. Unfortunately, there was not a complete understanding of the ancient Greek usage so there is no coherent path to be easily traced between ancient Greek usage and our present day nomenclature.

Using C Major as an example, we have the modes of the C Major scale :

- Ionian : the major scale starting on its tonic : C D E F G A B
- Dorian : starting on the second degree of the major scale : D E F G A B C
- Phrygian : starting on the third degree of the major scale : E F G A B C D
- Lydian : starting on the fourth degree of the major scale : F G A B C D E
- Mixolydian : starting on the fifth degree of the major scale : G A B C D E F
- Aeolian : starting on the sixth degree of the major scale : A B C D E F G
- Locrian : starting on the seventh degree of the major scale : B C D E F G A

If you try them on a piano, you will notice that each mode has a different feel. The changing position of the two semitone intervals (between E and F and between B and C) is what causes each mode to have a different sound although the notes are all the same.

There are several things to notice about these modes.

- All seven modes consist of the same set of seven notes
- They all have a perfect fifth interval between their tonic and their fifth degree with the exception of the Locrian mode where the interval between the tonic and the fifth degree is a tritone. Hence the tonic triad of Locrian mode is a diminished triad.

- Ionian, Lydian and Mixolydian are considered major modes because they have a major third interval between their tonic and third degrees.

- Dorian, Phrygian, Aeolian and Locrian are considered minor modes because they have a minor third interval between their tonic and third degrees.

- The Aeolian mode is the natural minor scale, the relative minor of the major scale at the origin of these modes ie. The relative minor of the Ionian mode.

- If a seventh chord is constructed on the tonic of the Mixolydian mode, it is a dominant seventh. It is the dominant seventh belonging to the scale one step round to the left on our circle of fifths. That is to say that the Mixolydian mode on G supplies on its tonic the dominant seventh chord of C Major. The Mixolydian mode can therefore be closely associated with the V of a ii-V-I chord progression.

## Which notes are in a given mode ?

To determine the set of notes to use in a mode, it is sufficient to remember on which degree of the major scale the mode starts. For example, if we have to decide which notes are represented by the mode of Mixolydian in D, we can follow this procedure :

- recall that the Mixolydian mode starts on the fifth degree of a major scale

- therefore, which major scale has D for its fifth degree ?

- this is the G Major scale

- which notes are in the G Major scale ?

- G A B C D E F♯

Our answer is therefore that :

D Mixolydian is the ordered set of notes : D E F♯ G A B C

## An alternative procedure

This has always seemed somewhat laborious to me but, happily, there is an alternative procedure. As we said on page 2, the major scale is used generally as the point of departure for determining chords and modes so to determine the set of notes in a given mode, we can start from the major scale having the same tonic and apply some rules.

Returning to the previous example where we needed the set of notes to be used with D Mixolydian, we can start from the D Major scale : D E F♯ G A B C♯. We see that the difference between D Major and D Mixolydian is that the one has a C♯ and the other has C for the seventh degree.

So the shortcut to decide which notes comprise D Mixolydian is to take D Major and flatten its seventh degree.

A similar set of rules can be used for each mode. The melodic analysis of each mode is given below as it relates to the major scale with the same tonic. The order of the modes has been changed to what I consider an easier order for remembering them – an order of increasing complexity.

- Lydian : 1 2 3 ♯4 5 6 7 (one extra sharp or one fewer flat)
- Mixolydian: 1 2 3 4 5 6 ♭7 (one extra flat or one fewer sharp)
- Dorian : 1 2 ♭3 4 5 6 ♭7 (two extra flats or two fewer sharps)
- Aeolian : 1 2 ♭3 4 5 ♭6 ♭7 (three " " " three " " )
- Phrygian : 1 ♭2 ♭3 4 5 ♭6 ♭7 (four " " " four " " )
- Locrian : 1 ♭2 ♭3 4 ♭5 ♭6 ♭7 (five " " " five " " )

As an example, consider E Phrygian which we have already seen above is E F G A B C D E (the third mode of C Major scale).

Compare this with the E Major scale : E F♯ G♯ A B C♯ D♯. If we flatten the 2nd, 3rd, 6th and 7th degrees, we obtain E F G A B C D which is exactly the E Phrygian mode.

Similarly, E Locrian requires flattening the 2nd, 3rd, 5th, 6th and 7th degrees of the E Major scale and this gives us E F G A B♭ C D as the notes of the E Locrian mode.

### *Rotational relationship of the modes.*

In the alternative procedure for determination of a given mode outlined above, the order given for the modes was described generally as one of increasing complexity. We might instead have said that it is an order in which the number of sharps is decreasing or the number of flats increasing.

On our circle, we are used to having the sharps decrease and flats increase with successive steps to the left, anti-clockwise. This is illustrated clearly in figure 15.6 which follows below.

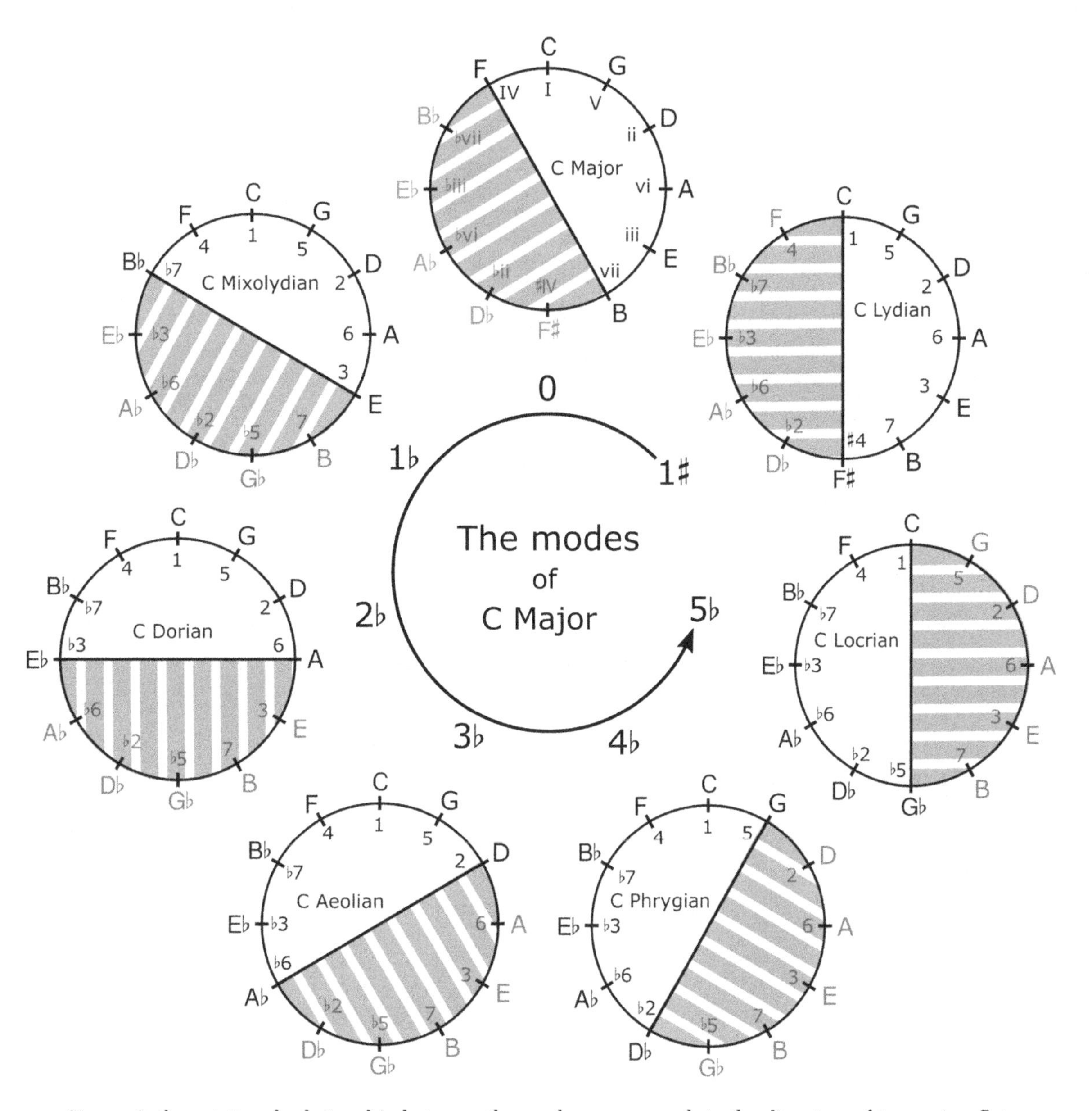


Figure 6: the rotational relationship between the modes corresponds to the direction of increasing flats

# Appendix D – illustration of the modes and 'inside' pentatonics

## Major modes

In chapter 10, Figure 10.10 showed the diatonic major scale on the circle of fifths and indicated that a pentatonic major scale can be constructed on the I, IV and V degrees of the scale.

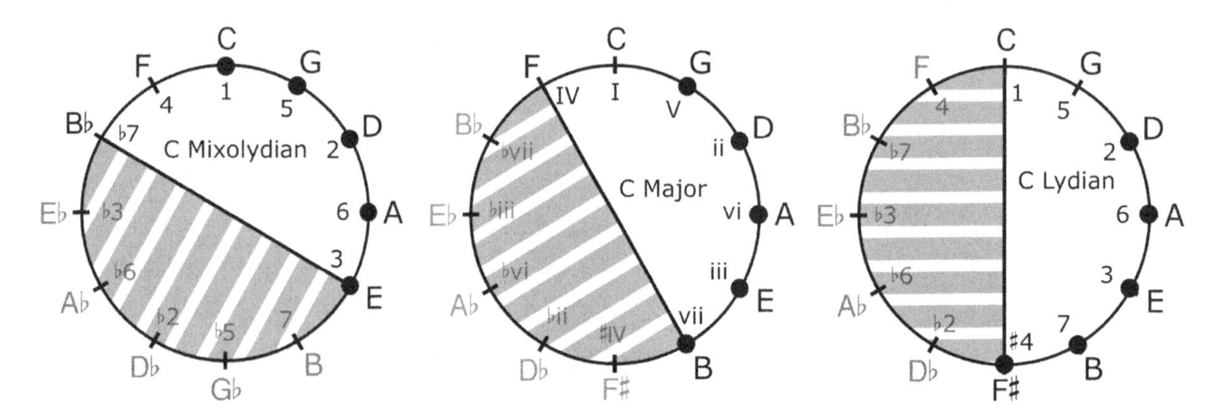


Figure 7: rotational relationship between the major modes of C Major

In Figure 15.7 you see that the same situation exists for all the traditional major modes : Ionian, Lydian, Mixolydian. It also shows the rotational relationship between these modes.

Three major pentatonic scales exist within each of these modes :

- in C Major, these are on the 1st, 4th and 5th degrees : C, F and G (G is shown with dots)
- in C Lydian, these are on the 1st, 2nd and 5th degrees : C, D and G (D is shown)
- in C Mixolydian, these are on the 1st, 4th and ♭7th degrees : C, F and B♭ (C is shown)

Also, note that C Lydian which has one more sharp (♯4) than C Major, is also rotated one step round to the right (clockwise) with respect to C Major. This corresponds with what we have already seen in Chapter 3 about the direction of increasing number of sharps.

Similarly, C Mixolydian which has one more flat (♭7) than C Major, is rotated one step round to the left (anti-clockwise) with respect to C Major. That is in the direction of increasing flats.

## Minor modes

Amongst the traditional modes, Dorian, Aeolian, Phrygian and Locrian are considered as minor modes. From Appendix C, we know that in comparison with a major scale, Dorian mode has 2 more flats, Aeolian has 3 more flats, Phrygian has 4 more flats and Locrian has five more flats.

Again when compared with a major scale, having the same tonic (see Figure 15.7), we may predict that the Dorian mode will be rotated 2 steps to the left; Aeolian 3 steps to the left, Phrygian 4 steps to the left and Locrian 5 steps to the left. Figure 15.8 shows this to be so.

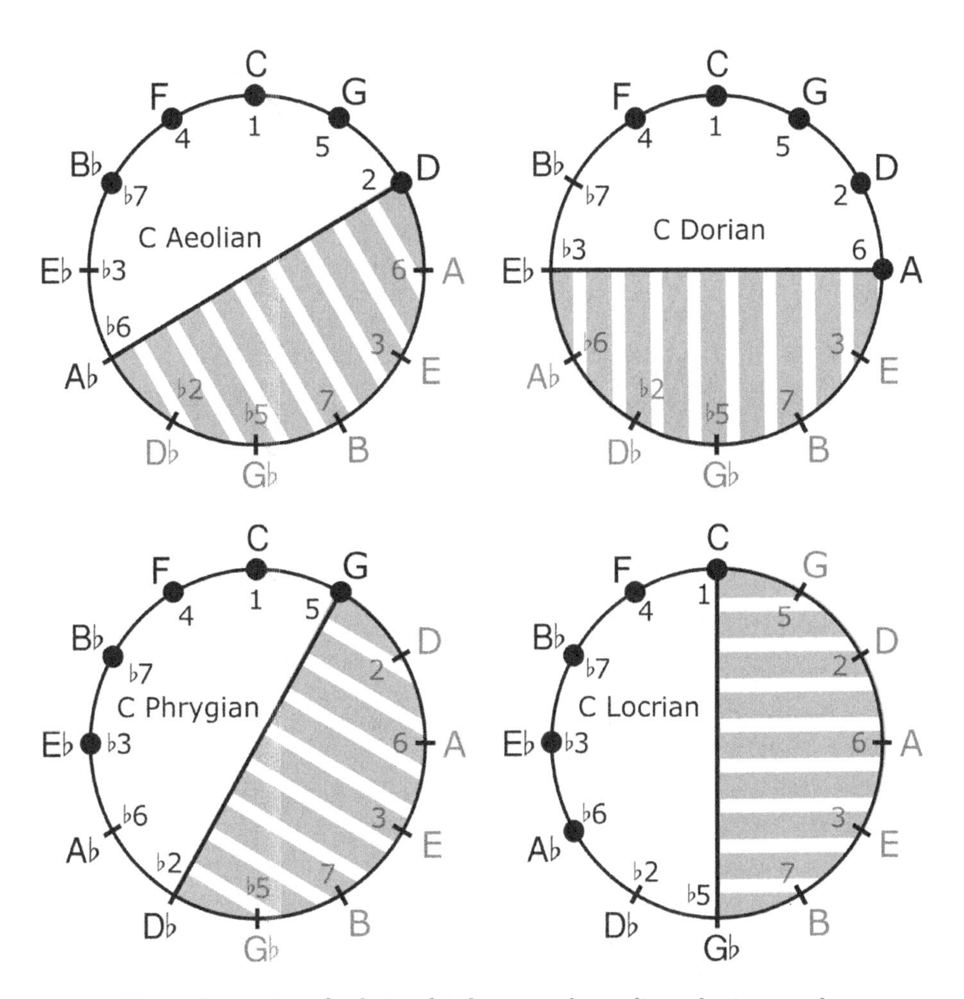


Figure 8: rotational relationship between the traditional minor modes

Each of these traditional minor modes contains three major pentatonic scales.

- in C Dorian, these are on the ♭$3^{rd}$, ♭$7^{th}$ and $4^{th}$ degrees : E♭, B♭ and F (F is shown with the dots)
- in C Aeolian, these are on the ♭$6^{th}$, ♭$3^{rd}$ and ♭$7^{th}$ degrees : A♭, E♭ and B♭ (B♭ is shown)
- in C Phrygian, these are on the ♭$2^{nd}$, ♭$6^{th}$ and ♭$3^{rd}$ degrees : D♭, A♭ and E♭ (E♭ is shown)
- in C Locrian, these are on the ♭$5^{th}$, ♭$2^{nd}$ and ♭$6^{th}$ degrees : G♭, D♭ and A♭ (A♭ is shown).

# Appendix E – Resources available for download

- A set of pages with blank circles for practice use : Blank-Circles.pdf
- A list of common transposing instruments : Transpos-instruments.pdf
- Notes on key signatures : Key-signatures.pdf
- A cheat sheet of simple intervals : Intervals-cheatsheet.pdf
- A cheat sheet of enharmonic equivalences for sharp keys and flat keys to help avoid double sharps and flats especially when transposing : Enharmonic-eq.pdf
- Another tool which will help avoid the complications of double sharps or flats is: Scale-spellings.pdf
- A cheat sheet on the harmonization of the major and minor scales : Harmonisations-of-the-scales.pdf

The above notices have been zipped into a single download available here :

https://le-theron.com/circle-resource/

## One last thing

If you have found this book useful for your progress in music, it would be helpful to other musicians and greatly appreciated by the author if you could leave a revue at :

https://www.amazon.com/review/create-review?&asin=B016WM7HZK

Thank you.

----- end -----

# General Index

Made in the USA
Las Vegas, NV
02 October 2021